THE SHAPING SPIRIT

The Shaping Spirit

A STUDY OF WALLACE STEVENS

BY

WILLIAM VAN O'CONNOR

NEW YORK

RUSSELL & RUSSELL · INC

1964

Manufactured in the United States of America

FOR MARY

A Prefatory Note

DESPITE ITS importance, the poetry of Wallace Stevens has not received critical attention of the kind lavished on the poetry of T. S. Eliot or W. B. Yeats. It may be too early, however, to attempt any full-scale examination. Although a few critics have recently begun to give his poetry more careful scrutiny, and many younger poets, as students of his work, are greatly in his debt, further detailed studies such as those undertaken by the late Hi Simons are needed before this definitive and exhaustive assessment will be possible. My purpose in publishing this examination will be served if it makes Stevens' poetry understandable in a fuller and more coherent way for those among his readers who have not had occasion to examine it in its entirety, or having read it entire wish to compare their understanding of it with that of another reader. My primary intention has been neither to eulogize nor place him neatly among his peers but, in his own words, "plainly to propound." There will be later books about him, written with a knowledge of his completed work and in the perspective of time.

No one can read through the entire body of Stevens' work to the present without being struck by the unusually rich sensibility and fine intelligence informing it. But the

same reader could on occasion feel that at crucial points
the thought meanders or turns in on itself. F. O. Matthiessen has made a similar observation: "Some of Stevens'
longer meditations may betray by their diffuseness of structure and the inconclusiveness of their thought his lonely
lack of interchange with other minds . . . ." Scattered throughout Stevens' work one will find such a statement as this: "It
seems that poetic order is potentially as significant as philosophical order." But shortly the poet in Stevens takes the
ascendancy and one observes him, as Plato might object,
imitating the flux, relating particulars in his brilliant fashion, making the concrete luminous. One cannot, for example, find as systematic an account of imagination in
Stevens as one can in such a work as R. G. Collingwood's
The Principles of Art. Yet one finds many statements about
the way imagination functions, in the creation of metaphor,
of style, of systems of architecture, of love, of heroes, or of
nobility. Stevens, unlike Collingwood, does not trace the
history of philosophical theories of imagination nor state his
own theory in any definitive fashion. He does, however,
discuss contemporary attitudes toward imagination and point
out statements made by philosophers and estheticians with
which he agrees or disagrees. Perhaps in the long run
Stevens' own imaginative expressions and his discussions
of the uses of imagination will be of more value than a neat
statement of the exact differentiations between imagination
and the other faculties of the mind.

One may also remark the singleness of purpose and subject matter in Stevens' work. *Harmonium* appeared when
Stevens was forty-four, considerably older than most poets
publishing a first book. There is therefore a remarkable con-
sistency among his books despite the enlargement and qualifications he has been able to bring to his subject matter. A
certain amount of repetitiousness seems small enough payment for the depth, firmness and complexity his singleness

of subject matter and of purpose have enabled him to achieve.

For many comments and suggestions that helped me greatly in the preparation of this study I am indebted to Leonard Unger, Cleanth Brooks, Robert Penn Warren, Danforth Ross and Theodore Hornberger. My debt to my wife, Mary Allen O'Connor, is suggested, however inadequately, by the dedication. Parts of the study appeared, in somewhat different forms, in *Perspective, University of Kansas City Review* and *The Western Review*. I am grateful to the editors of these magazines for permission to use the material here.

W. V. O'C.

University of Minnesota
Minneapolis, Minnesota

TABLE OF CONTENTS

THE SHAPING SPIRIT

I

Stevens as Legend

WALLACE STEVENS has engaged the imaginations of his
fellow poets on many scores, not least that he has been an
insurance lawyer with, and since 1934 a vice president of,
the Hartford Accident and Indemnity Company. In our
time the alienation of the poet from his society has been a
frequently observed phenomenon. And perhaps a mark or
a consequence of this alienation has been the gathering of
poets into groups or into schools. One of the strains in the
pattern of alienation, of course, is that of the Symbolists, to
whom Stevens as a poet is greatly indebted. William York
Tindall has written wittily about the spirit of exile, or
alienation, that informs a good deal of modern poetry, including Stevens' own:

> To be exiled or even unsociably fashionable requires a
> society. The society which expelled these literary exiles and
> gave them their manners is of course that of the middle
> class, which from early in the nineteenth century has been
> increasingly hostile or indifferent to poets. Accustomed to
> expressing feelings and ideas shared with their literate audi-
> ence, poets slowly realized their disinclination or inability
> to express feelings so much coarser than their own. About
> the middle of the century Baudelaire looked out his window

and was filled with the "immense nausea of billboards." The
rest follows from this.

No poet has written more subtly about his feelings and his
ideas than Stevens, and no poet of his genius has been
more steadily ignored by the large middle-class audiences.
Stevens has been

> The poet striding among the cigar stores,
> Ryan's lunch, hatters, insurance and medicine

writing about

> hero-hymns
> Chorals for mountain voices and the moral chant. . . .

> Hymns of the struggle of the idea of god
> And the idea of man, the mystic garden and
> The middling beast, the garden of paradise
> And he that created the garden and peopled it.

There is nothing especially strange about a poet like Stevens dividing his life between insurance and poetry. Other
poets also live in the middle-class world, as doctors or teach-
ers or employees in publishing houses. They manage to live
like Stevens with a foot in each world, but he, a great poet
and a successful insurance man, seems to dramatize in an
ironic fashion the break between the world of the poet and
the world of business. Also the substance and manner of his
poetry appear incongruous against the middle-class business
world in which Stevens has lived.

Stevens' work represents, in certain ways, a nineteenth-
century estheticism, particularly as this was expressed in Mallarmé, Verlaine, and Laforgue. But this is true, in various
ways, of Eliot, Pound, the Sitwells, Aiken or Tate. Stevens in
his own way and for his own purposes and subject learned

how to employ the language of ambiguity, the modulated tones of stressed and unstressed sounds, evocative rhythms, the shifts of light and shadow, the interaction of theme and symbol, and the mysterious luminousness of metaphor newly caught. Controlling the elegance of his lines are a rich sensibility and a wonderfully quick intelligence. And the subjects about which he has written have public value.

The world of *Harmonium* is rich, almost effete. It is a world of comfortable living, *objets d'art*, voyages in the Caribbean, French phrases, sophisticated knowledge and wit. If it indicates little or no awareness of political and economic problems, it exhibits none the less a humane, intelligent awareness, a searching for a principle of integrity and order. Crispin, in the long poem "The Comedian as the Letter C," searches for a way of life that will satisfy his intelligence. He accepts the society and the region he knows. And he compromises with the achievements possible to him as a poet for the satisfactions open to him as a man. But there is no closing of the mind to the forces that in their eccentricity had made the society he liked. These forces, he says in "Tea at the Palace of Hoon," also had made him. The mystery and the terror of these forces are real—but so is the tea we sip in our secure little rooms.

> I was the world in which I walked, and what I saw
> Or heard or felt came not but from myself;
> And there I found myself more truly and more strange.

The "burghers," Stevens' unimaginative men of commerce, live in their security, but "The Doctor of Geneva" is aware of the heavens and the "ruinous waste." His mind simmered

> Until the steeples of his city clanked and sprang
> In an unburgherly apocalypse.
> The doctor used his handkerchief and sighed.

We are "dark comedians." One cannot afford to write too
many "tragic testaments," but even in the midst of his successes the sensitive man, as in "Banal Sojourn," ponders,
mildly ironic:

> One has a malady, here, a malady. One feels a malady.

The mysterious firmament has its earthly counterparts, especially the sea.

> There will never be an end
> To this droning of the surf

Crispin finds it an "inscrutable world." When the pro-
tagonist of "From the Misery of Don Joost" finishes his
"combat with the sun," his body, "the old animal," is free
from all knowledge, all experience. In "Valley Candle" the
image is of a candle burning brightly in a valley—"Until
the wind blew." This, then, is the world, from primitive to
social and esthetic, that is found in *Harmonium*. It is a
world with which one must come to terms.

Stevens' way of coming to terms with it is to understand
the imagination. In "Colloquy with a Polish Aunt" we read,
"Imagination is the will of things." In "To the One of Fictive Music" the prayerful request is to return to us "The
imagination that we spurned and crave." We must, through
the agency of the imagination, impose order on the wilderness, just as the jar in "Anecdote of the Jar" imposes its
order:

> It made the slovenly wilderness
> Surround that hill.

Perhaps Stevens' purpose is caught best of all in "Homunculus et la Belle Étoile." The star is a good light for poets,

drunkards and young women soon to be married—the light
of beauty and thoughtfulness.

> It is a good light, then, for those
> That know the ultimate Plato,
> Tranquillizing with this jewel
> The torments of confusion.

There are probably very few poems written in English
in the twentieth century comparable in their exquisite
beauty to "Sunday Morning," "The Snow Man," "Le Monocle de Mon Oncle," "Of the Manner of Addressing
Clouds," "Of Heaven Considered as a Tomb," "Peter
Quince at the Clavier," and "Cortège for Rosenbloom." In
the urbane manner Jonson and Herrick seem to be ante-
cedents; in the simple but great dignity, Milton; in the
wonderful ambiguity of words and "floating images," Mallarmé; and in the ironic detachment, Laforgue. Even though
some of these similarities may not or should not suggest actual "influences," they must be noted in order to suggest
the range and tone of the language of these poems. The
precise diction and the interconnected body of imagery and
symbols seem to be solely Stevens' own. And all of these
characteristics are caught and held in a consciousness or
awareness that is "contemporaneous."

Stevens has also been a somewhat mysterious figure to
his fellow poets because he has, for the most part, gone his
own way. He has felt no deep need for frequent or close
personal associations with other writers. But these writers
have long looked upon him as a poet's poet, as the exquisite
and careful artist.

In 1926, when he was already something of a legend,
Harriet Monroe recalled her first awareness of Wallace
Stevens:

The War Number of *Poetry* was in page proof when his
series of *Phases* arrived, compelling the editors to squeeze
an extra two pages into the make-up—a last minute conces-
sion which sufficed for only four of the six or seven battle
sketches in the group. To this day the others have never
been published; indeed, *Fallen Winkle*, reprinted in *The
New Poetry*, is the only poem of the series which the
author has permitted to appear.

In 1914 Stevens, then thirty-five, was practicing law in
New York City. During the following year he contributed
to the Greenwich Village *Rogue*, a little semimonthly magazine edited by Louise and Allan Norton which lasted for
slightly more than half a year, while he was associated with
some of its contributors, Carl Van Vechten, Donald Evans,
Walter Arensberg, and Mina Loy. In 1916 he moved to
Hartford. From this point on, the legend around Stevens
grew. Alfred Kreymborg, who as anthologist and critic has
been one of the most ardent of Stevens' supporters, is
among those responsible for nurturing it.

Kreymborg met Stevens at a tea given by the Nortons.
Subsequently, as editor of *Others*, which began in July
1915, he published a considerable number of Stevens'
poems, including "Peter Quince at the Clavier," "Domination of Black," and "Six Significant Landscapes." In his
autobiography, *Troubadour* (1925), Kreymborg recalled
Stevens' visits to New York from Hartford:

> The occasions he came down from Hartford . . . he devoted
> to pedestrianism around New York and invited Krimmie to
> join him. So slight was Krimmie alongside Wallace that the
> latter was fond of guiding him against the traffic. On one of
> these walks, the giant suddenly stuffed a package into his
> editorial pocket, with the hasty proviso: "I must ask you not
> to breathe a word about this. Print it if you like it, send it

back if you don't." It was the manuscript—in the most minute handwriting—of the now famous poem, Peter Quince at the Clavier.

Stevens undoubtedly visited New York City after his removal to Hartford and undoubtedly took these walks with Kreymborg, but since "Peter Quince" was published in the second issue of *Others*, August 1915, and Stevens did not leave New York for Hartford until 1916, it seems likely that it was some other poem that Stevens stuffed into Kreymborg's pocket. But the legend is helped if we can think it was this poem which has been anthologized many, many times and has come to typify Stevens' characteristic artistry. The anecdote also thickens the shadow behind which Stevens, the poet who insists on being a private man, is said to live.

For Stevens, publishing a book of poems was a serious matter. In a letter to William Carlos Williams, a friend from his New York City days, Stevens wrote that he thought discipline for the poet involved discovering one's "particular quality" and then developing this quality "in intensity and volume." There is also in the letter, which Williams printed in his *Kora in Hell* (1920), this sentence, which has been frequently repeated by reviewers of Stevens' volumes of poetry: "Well a book of poems is a damned serious affair."

In 1922 Miss Amy Lowell published anonymously *A Critical Fable*. By this date the image of Stevens as careless and half indifferent to his great gifts existed commonly enough in the myths created by literary gossips to allow her to account for him in these terms:

There's another young man who strums a clavier
And prints a new poem every third or fourth year.

Looking back, I don't know that anything since
Has delighted me more than his *Peter Quince*.
He has published no book and adopts this as pose,
But it is rather more likely I think to suppose
The particular gift he's received from the Muses
Is a tufted green field under whose grass there oozes
A seeping of poetry, like wind through a cloister;
On occasion it rises, and then the field's moister
And he has a poem he'll trouble to bale it,
Address it to *Poetry* and afterwards mail it.
His name, though the odds overbalance the evens
Of those who don't know it as yet's Wallace Stevens,
But it might be John Doe for all he seems to care—
A little fine work scattered into the air
By the wind it appears, and he quite unaware
Of the fact, since his motto's a cool 'laisser faire.'

Miss Lowell had first become aware of Stevens' work when
she read the second issue of *Others*. "Who is Mr. Stevens?"
she had written to Kreymborg. "His things have an ex-
traordinarily imaginative tang. That 'Silver Plough-Boy' is
quite delightful, though no better than 'Peter Quince at
the Clavier'. . . . But who is Mr. Stevens? Tell me something about him." The refusal to publish a book would
seem less a pose than a concern to get his own "special quality" in sufficient quantity. The "Silver Plough-Boy," which
Miss Lowell admired, was allowed to appear in the first edition of *Harmonium*, but it was dropped from the second
edition.

Miss Monroe was responsible not only for introducing
Stevens to the poetry-reading world but also for assisting in
the growth of the legend. The first version of "Sunday
Morning" appeared in *Poetry* in November 1915, and in
June of the same year the editors awarded Stevens a $100
contest prize for the verse play, "Three Travellers Watch a

Sunrise." Miss Monroe stressed several elements of the legend: Stevens' sudden arrival in the literary world not merely as a fully matured poet but as a poet of genius, his all but excessive perfectionism, and his personal impressiveness. In her autobiography, *A Poet's Life* (1938), she quoted from a letter Arthur Ficke wrote her in 1915 after he had read "Sunday Morning":

> Have you ever known Stevens? He's a big, slightly fat, awfully competent looking man. You expect him to roar, but when he speaks there emerges the gravest, softest, most subtly modulated voice I've ever heard—a voice on tiptoe at dawn!

But it is Kreymborg who, also insisting on Stevens' genius, has most insisted on the legend. "The Hartford lawyer is contemptuous of worldly popularity," Kreymborg wrote in *Our Singing Strength* (1929). "For years his friends had begged him to publish a book, and Stevens, bored with being the sole poet who had refused to publish a book, permitted Carl Van Vechten to cajole Alfred Knopf into printing *Harmonium*. Comparatively few copies were sold; the rest remaindered." In the same passage Kreymborg adds several strokes for the sake of the legendary figure:

> Formerly, it was impossible to get him to publish a book; now it is impossible to get him to publish a poem. Write him, wire him or visit him, one always receives the same answer: he has written nothing for years. . . . [One] waits in vain for the fist of the Connecticut giant to scratch off another perfect etching. . . . Continued self-deprecation has finally removed the man from the scene in which he always refused to participate.

Then after some appreciative and incisive comments on the nature of Stevens' poetry Kreymborg is busy at the legend again:

The man is a little weary of insurance cases, clients and courts, opposing lawyers and judges. He decides on a short vacation, not among friends and not among Parisians, but among the Carolinas, or better still, down in Ponce de Leon's Florida. In between delectable meals and wines, if wines there be, one gets rid of the itch of thinking. If some editorial friend is idiotic enough to demand these notes, let him have them, and the less said the better. But enough of such nonsense, no more nonsense henceforth.

Van Vechten, apparently, has not referred in print to his part in getting *Harmonium* published. In his "Notes for an Autobiography," published in *Colophon* in 1930, he mentioned Stevens only as a contributor to a "dying magazine of parts" which he once edited.

Despite the lack of popular support for or knowledge of his poetry, Stevens' reputation grew steadily with the critics and with the poets. There was a lapse of roughly six years following the publication of *Harmonium* during which he wrote almost nothing for publication, but then he began as before to contribute fairly steadily to the little magazines.

Meanwhile the legend also grew. In 1940 Charles Henri Ford could use as a subtitle for an article in *View* this question: "Has the Mystery Man of Modern Poetry Really Another Self?" And by 1946 the legend received a kind of official sanction in the *Saturday Review of Literature*. This is the opening paragraph of an article by Will Vance entitled "Wallace Stevens: Man Off the Street":

Wallace Stevens, born in Reading, Pennsylvania, October 2, 1879, remains the Lone Wolf of American Poetry. Men of letters, some of them prominent, and visiting firemen with gilt edged introductions have stormed his Hartford fortress in vain—or to their deep regret. And woe to the autograph hunter!

We find it necessary, as Stevens himself well knows, to create legends. A man or an experience that has become a legend lives in our mind in luminous significance. Mere facts, delimited and carefully divorced from feeling, destroy not merely our feeling about them but their significance; they become fixed and dead. A legend grows that we may isolate special qualities. It has its origin and its best reason for being in our need for perceiving the exact identity, in Stevens' own words, "the precise line and look," of the man or experience that engages our imaginations. We enjoy the special qualities and we try to grasp their significance. Stevens the man and the poet became a legend because in him the complex pattern of alienation found a personification.

Relatively little of Stevens' private life is known. He was born in 1879 to Garrett Barckalow Stevens, a lawyer, and Mary Catherine (Zeller) Stevens. His ancestry was Dutch. Stevens has made relatively few explicit references to his origins. There is, to be sure, the fine poem "Dutch Graves in Bucks County," and also "The Bed of Old John Zeller." In his article "About One of the Poems of Marianne Moore's" he recounts a visit to the "old Zeller house in Tulpehocken, in Pennsylvania." He refers to the family, which came to America in 1709, as "religious refugees." But he writes about the Zeller family not as his ancestors but to illustrate a point he is making concerning one's sense of reality. The people and the experiences are transmuted and become impersonal, like the figure of Grandfather John Zeller when he is used to illustrate the ease with which our forebears could give themselves to their beliefs. When asked by Charles Henri Ford about his early associations, Stevens said he had a high-school friend with whom he talked about poetry. The friend used to recite poetry as they were walking "through the woods—very loud. Very clear."

At Harvard, Stevens went on to say, he wrote a little verse. In "The Wallace Stevens Number" of *The Harvard Advocate* (Dec., 1940) there are thirteen poems (some of them under such pseudonyms as "R. Jerries" and "Henry Marshall") written during his three years at Harvard, 1897–1900. In 1904, after graduation from New York Law School, he was admitted to the bar. He told Ford that he did not take his undergraduate verse very seriously. He wanted to be a lawyer, a successful one; he "wanted material success, wife, home, comfort—all that he has." Later on, when he was practicing law in New York City, he associated with some of his college friends who were writing or painting. "Greenwich Village was budding, blooming." The poems, one after another, were written down—but he had no plans for a literary career or even for a book. After the publication of *Harmonium,* he said, "poetry was forgotten, more or less. Business of being a corporation lawyer; advancement. But poetry came back, intermittently, in spite of himself."

Stevens had also worked briefly for the *Herald Tribune* after his graduation from law school. Few or none of Stevens' later associates knew him at this time, but William Carlos Williams has recalled that subsequently there were various stories about him, one of them quite contrary to the later legend, with its elements of spectacular success. These are Williams' own words:

> There is also the story of the down and out Stevens sitting on a park bench at the Battery watching the outgoing tide and thinking to join it, as a corpse, on its way to the sea (he had been a failure as a reporter). As he sat there watching the debris floating past him he began to write—noting the various articles as they passed. He became excited as he wrote and ended by taking to the Tribune office an editorial

or "story" that has become famous—in a small way among newspaper offices. . . .

Williams also has a strong recollection of Stevens in relation to the writers he had known before moving to Hartford. Again, these are Williams' own words:

> Stevens kept up his acquaintance with the entire New York group—Kreymborg, Arensberg, Marianne Moore, Lola Ridge, myself, even Cummings—coming to New York on several occasions to parties, meetings, but always in a distant manner, shyly, unwilling to be active or vocal. Everybody knew him, knew him well—but he never said much. He was always the well dressed one, diffident about letting down his hair. Precise when we were sloppy. Drank little. . . . But we all knew, liked and admired him. He really was felt to be part of the gang.

Between 1914 and 1923, when *Harmonium* was issued, Stevens published about 100 poems in magazines like *Secession, Broom, The New Republic, The Measure, The Little Review, Contact, The Soil,* and *The Modern School.* His second verse play, the one-act *Carlos among the Candles,* was taken to New York by the Wisconsin Players, who had performed it in Milwaukee. In 1920 the Provincetown Players, with Edna Millay as heroine, performed *Three Travellers Watch a Sunrise,* his first play. The drama critics poked fun at *Carlos* and ignored *Three Travellers.* But his success with his poems continued. *Poetry* awarded him the Levinson Prize in 1920 and *The Dial* in 1922 presented him as a distinguished contributor. Yet *Harmonium,* which contained 74 poems, a few never before printed, but omitted about 25 which had appeared in magazines, sold fewer than a hundred copies. There was high praise in reviews by Marianne Moore and Matthew Josephson and

recognition by Mark Van Doren of Stevens' relationship
with the poetry of Eliot, Pound and Robert Graves. A few
reviewers found *Harmonium* precious, exotic, or superfine
—that is, with qualities that would prevent its winning
wide approval.[1]

Quite likely the poor reception given *Harmonium* played
a strong part in Stevens' temporary neglect of poetry for
business. In 1924 he published "Sea Surface Full of Clouds"
in *The Dial* and "Red Loves Kit" in *The Measure*. The former seems now to be generally accepted as one of the most
beautiful poems composed in the twentieth century. Then
for six years he published nothing. Despite his silence,
Stevens' reputation increased greatly between 1924 when
Llewellyn Powys and Gorham Munson wrote apprecia-
tively of him and 1929 when Allen Tate in *The Bookman*
called him "the most finished poet of the age." In 1930
poems began to appear again, and in the following year
Harmonium was reissued.[2]

In 1935 *Ideas of Order*[3] appeared. *Harmonium* had
been misunderstood by many American readers and critics
because it represented a world of esthetic concerns. If the
symbolism and *objets d'art* had represented a less individu-
alized sensibility these concerns might have been seen more

---

[1] In "Vicissitudes of Reputation, 1914–1940," *The Harvard Advocate*, Dec. 1940, Hi Simons has traced the critical reception of Stevens'
earlier books.

[2] New York, Alfred A. Knopf, 1931. In this second edition fourteen
poems were added and three appearing in the first edition were dropped.
It should be noted that Stevens made changes in some of his poems for
Harmonium. For example, "Sunday Morning," I–IV, in Miss Monroe's
The New Poetry, 1917, is different from "Sunday Morning," V–VIII,
in *Harmonium*, 1923; and *The New Republic*, Sept. 14, 1921, version
of "The Man Whose Pharynx Was Bad" differs from the *Harmonium*
version. These changes suggest the care which Stevens has always given
to his work.

[3] New York, Alcestis Press. Republished by Alfred A. Knopf, 1936.
Six poems which had appeared in the magazines between 1929 and
1935 were excluded.

clearly in the way Stevens saw them, as spiritual expressions of a philosophy and way of life. But America had inherited the fatuous notion that an esthetic emphasis and the posings of Oscar Wilde and some of his fellows were the same thing. Reality, it seemed, was the elephantine weight of Dreiser, the street idiom of Sandburg, or some expression of the political and economic crisis. *Ideas of Order* is composed of poems that bring the sensibility and intelligence responsible for the distinguished and subtle elegance of *Harmonium* into focus against the preconceptions and preoccupations that had kept many readers from understanding and sympathizing with that book. In the opening poem of *Ideas of Order*, "Sailing After Lunch," Stevens acknowledged himself

> A most inappropriate man
> In a most unpropitious place.

The poem, somewhat flat in tone, mildly ridicules the then still current myth that the objective-historical fact alone is true, that the way one views it or feels about it is somehow untrue—the hoary Hobbesian fallacy of the antithesis between objective-fact-and-laws and subjective-individual-views-and-feelings about it. "Meditations Celestial and Terrestrial" continues the protest against this oversimplification, against what John Crowe Ransom called the failure to accept the world as body. We have striven to live by the

> bluest reason
> In a world of wind and frost.

In terms of Stevens' personal use of *blue* the phrase "bluest reason" has a double meaning; it signifies the life-of-reason which, alone, makes for cold and icy existence, but it also

suggests that the delimited little myth of truth-as-objective-
fact is also a way of seeing an imagined, though limited,
version of the world. Stevens finds this view inadequate:

> But what are radiant reason and radiant will
> To warblings early in the hilarious trees
> Of summer, the drunken mother?

And, for those who incline to believe that reality must be
harsh as well as solid, there is the little note in "Like Decorations in a Nigger Cemetery":

> Crow is realist. But, then,
> Oriole, also, may be realist.

There are also poems indicating the pressures exerted
upon Stevens' mind by politics and economics. "Mozart,
1935" and "Botanist on Alp (No. 1)" acknowledge the economic ills which cause some to want to dismiss poetry as a
luxury, or to ignore the graces to be seen in Nature. In
these subjects, he would find enough to occupy him for his
next two volumes, *Owl's Clover* and *The Man With the
Blue Guitar & Other Poems*. But there is also in *Ideas of
Order,* as the title seems to suggest, a sense of alarm over
the disintegration of an inherited order and its beliefs:

> The epic of disbelief
> Blares oftener and soon, will soon be constant.

And there are tentative pencilings that suggest the direction and the concepts underlying them of the more considered ideas-of-order to be developed in the later books. In
"Lions in Sweden" he says we hanker after "sovereign
images," after symbols that are informed by our beliefs. If
those we have inherited—Fides, Justitia, Patentia, and For-

titudo—no longer serve us we can and will create others. In "The Idea of Order at Key West" we learn that the world we "see" is the only world there is for us; and because of his "rage for order" the poet, like us, strives to create a coherent and beautiful order through his words. And in "Academic Discourse at Havana" he observes the passing or partial passing of the order he has known:

> And a grand decadence settles down like cold.

Ideas of Order exhibits a partially different poet from the one who wrote *Harmonium*. In the first book there is the elegance of a world that, for Stevens at least, had not been seriously questioned. In *Ideas of Order* it is questioned. The language of the poetry, adjusting itself to the new subjects, becomes less imagistic and more direct, and the subjects become increasingly theoretical and abstract. *Ideas of Order* is the beginning of an important shift in Stevens' career, inaugurating his turning from subjects for poetry to a consideration of poetry itself as it relates to the role of imagination in a world of shifting values. In "Sad Strains of a Gay Waltz" he says:

> Too many waltzes are ended. And then
> There's that mountain-minded Hoon.

Two other books appeared during the 1930's, *Owl's Clover* (1936)[4] and *The Man With the Blue Guitar & Other Poems* (1937). All of them reflect the political tensions of the decade. The bulk of the work would imply some such feeling on Stevens' part as he later made explicit in talking to Ford: "Now that I am getting older I am more jealous of the demands business makes—I should like to de-

[4] New York, Alcestis Press. Reprinted in revised form with *The Man with the Blue Guitar & Other Poems*, New York, Alfred A. Knopf.

vote more—all—of my time to the study and writing of poetry." All through Stevens' career there has been an intense desire to understand the nature of poetry and to give the utmost care to the writing of it. In 1948 when the question of publishing his collected prose pieces was under discussion he concluded the matter in these words: "I ought not to publish a book of prose until I have put as much thought and care into every line of it as I would put into a book of poetry." During the 1940's he has continued to publish frequently. There have been *Parts of a World* (1942),[5] *Notes toward a Supreme Fiction* (1942),[6] *Esthétique du Mal* (1942),[7] *Transport to Summer* (1947),[8] *Three Academic Pieces* (1947)[9] and *A Primitive Like an Orb* (1948).[10]

Stevens has lived apart from other poets. How much this has been accidental, the result of his working among men with little interest in poetry, or intentional, an unwillingness to make his private life public, it seems hard to decide. He did say, in 1940, that for years his poetry was a kind of "secret vice," but he added that it was no longer secret—"I don't care anymore."

That men of letters, as Will Vance said, "stormed his Hartford fortress in vain—or to their deep regret" is undoubtedly an exaggeration. And the "woe to the autograph hunter" seems an unnecessary touch since hardly any of the readers of Stevens' poetry would be ardent collectors of autographs. In comparison with other men of letters he has lived in sufficient isolation to give rise as late as 1940 to such statements as Fred B. Millett's in *Contemporary*

[5] Alfred A. Knopf.
[6] Cummington Press.
[7] *Idem.*
[8] Alfred A. Knopf. This volume includes *Notes toward a Supreme Fiction* and *Esthétique du Mal*.
[9] Cummington Press.
[10] Gotham Book Mart.

American Authors: "His retirement and infrequent publication has made Stevens almost a myth to other poets." It is hardly true that he has published infrequently. In comparison with that of most other modern poets the bulk of his work is considerable. On the other hand, for such publications as *Who's Who* he has furnished only the barest essentials, such as "married, one daughter, Holly Bright," the titles of his books, and his official business connections. Even the autobiographical "The Comedian as the Letter C," though apparently true to the spirit of Stevens' relationship to the craft of poetry, is hardly true to the literal fact:

> Four daughters in a world too intricate . . .
> Four questioners and four sure answerers.

From the very first, however, he has taken poetry seriously. That he did not look upon himself, and may not even now so look upon himself, as a greatly gifted poet, and therefore obligated to follow a career in literature alone, is something quite distinct from being indifferent to poetry.

In recent years Stevens has become more of a public figure. He continues as a vice president of the Accident and Indemnity Company, but he has given a number of public lectures and occasionally the Hartford newspapers mention him in his role as poet. To the academic world and to the readers of modern poetry he is increasingly well known and more and more looked upon as one of the greatest poets in the language. Stevens as legend remains an interesting, even a symbolic, figure. In his own person he dramatizes the opposition between the world of business and the alienated artist. In his poetry the careful craftsmanship of the symbolists, who most strongly opposed the values of the bourgeois world, finds its best American expression. Despite his success in the world of affairs he has remained aloof in

the sense that he has been an observer, a man who would
have his world more aware of its own preconceptions, of
the nature of imagination, or of the past:

> He rode over Connecticut
> In a glass coach.
> Once a fear pierced him,
> In that he mistook
> The shadow of his equipage
> For blackbirds.

And he can write a difficult poem about the subtle nature
of the imagination but end it with ironic detachment:

> Goodbye,
> Mrs. Pappadopoulos, and thanks.

II

Imagined Reality

IN RECENT years Stevens has come to be recognized as an American poet of the rank of Eliot. Actually Stevens and Eliot are comparable only in terms of their skill. Their idioms, themes and major interests are sufficiently dissimilar to discourage any explicit comparisons. Temperamentally the two men are different. Perhaps they are best characterized, providing neither term is used in any pejorative or absolute sense, as hedonist and as ascetic. Both poets are concerned with the nature of poetry and the role of the poet or artist. Both are concerned with belief, ideals and morality. But the major theme in Stevens by which these concerns are organized is the nature of imagination and its relation to "reality," while the major theme in Eliot is the need for a stable society, having traditional religious and cultural forms and values.

In "The Noble Rider and the Sound of Words," an excellent critical essay, Stevens says that we in the twentieth century are the victims of an obsession. We pride ourselves on being willing to face the facts. With Bertrand Russell, we, as free men, take a cold, ironic pleasure in living in an alien universe. If our "naturalistic" literature and our tendency to read "escapism" for imagination are indicative of

the contemporary mind, we seem determined not to allow
the imagination either to help reconcile us to the facts or to
transform them. Stevens does not shy away at the mention
of romanticism. Therein, he says, may lie our salvation.

Such statements as these necessarily offend many contemporary minds. When Stevens cries "jargon" or "cant"
upon meeting indiscriminate use of terms like "escapist" or
"realist," these same minds are likely to dismiss him with
another label, "obscurantist," to dismiss him as a victim of
the general failure of nerve. When we look more closely
into his beliefs, however, we find that Stevens' concern that
we recognize the place of the imagination does not have as
its counterpart any admonition that we should deny the
presence, nature or importance of "things-as-they-are."

In one of his earlier poems, "The Comedian as the Letter C," Stevens says he would see the world as the "stiffest
realist" sees it. To those who remind him that man's life
ends in darkness and dissolution, nothing more, he can
point to these lines:

> casual flocks of pigeons make
> Ambiguous undulations as they sink
> Downward to darkness, on extended wings.

If he is reminded of the universe as mechanism he can note
that he has observed for himself

> the clanking mechanism
> Of machine within machine within machine.

He admits, too, in "Theory," "Anecdote of Men by the
Thousand," and "The Latest Freed Man," the awesome
power of environment. Undoubtedly, if the theme had
stirred him, there would be a proper acknowledgment of
environment's twin, heredity. Again, he would acknowl-

edge that man seems a chance phenomenon given life by the same impersonal forces that nourish the tree and allow species to become extinct. Stevens would deny no such bitter postulates, which many see as forced upon us by nineteenth-century science. But he would *add* that the mind is creative, that it struggles to control and dominate the world.

The modern mind, however, tends, to use Yeats' term, to be passive, to be in awe of objective fact. We do, for example, have a style but it tends to be skeptical, tentative and noncommittal. And sometimes it aspires to be photographic. We emphasize our sense of disruption and disorganization. We have come to mistrust the imagination itself. Stevens, by implication, reminds us that however dull the tones in which we see the world we are seeing it imaginatively. If we create such a somber style we are cheating ourselves. The imagination can serve us well, if we grant it certain freedoms and learn how it creates. It can create a style, one informed by exuberance, aspiration and a resilient spirit, which at once sustains and expresses human dignity.

Every culture has a style, a way of expressing its motivating spirit. If that spirit is leaden and weighted down by a belief that the imagination should not be allowed to transform the surface of experience the style of the culture will lack exuberance and resilience. It will exhibit the heavy spirit that is its informing power. Certainly the style of the Elizabethans is caught quite as distinctly in their pageantry, in their jeweled clothing and in their political maneuvers as in the rhetoric of their plays, just as the style of the Victorians is caught in their furniture, their clothing and their manners. It seems just, if somewhat ironic, that although the style of a culture exposes its informing spirit, the culture itself is responsible for the style through its control of and attitude toward the imagination. At the close of "Le

Monocle de Mon Oncle," Stevens feigns surprise that "flut-
tering things"—the things of the imagination—"have so distinct a shade." The shade, in our terms, is the style of the
culture. The degree of freedom for the imagination has its
ultimate significance in the very character of the culture.

Again, more is involved than the externals—architecture,
clothing or furniture—of a culture, important as these are.
We as individuals, with styles, or, more fashionably, with
personalities, create a part of the world in which we live.
Our sense of the appropriate or of the beautiful dictates, as
it were, the nature and the limitations of that style. In one
poem, "Add This to Rhetoric," while noting the importance of individual style—

> In the way you speak
> You arrange, the thing is posed—

Stevens observes also that human expressions, style, will
not keep the sun from rising. But we should not therefore
neglect the importance of style.

Holding to his major theme, the relation between imagination and reality as coequals, Stevens has moved beyond a
concern with esthetics (although he was never, as he has
been called, a "pure poet") to a concern with the relationship between imagination and humanistic ideals, morality
and belief. Like many of the other moderns, as we have
noted, Stevens finds the old beliefs "obsolete." Even though
we have lost "the idea of god," we are free to substitute an
"idea of man." We may still aspire. "The philosopher's
man still walks in dew"—man may realize his "fictions."
But Stevens is never naïve. He is not asking that the poet
project filmy ideals and proceed to live within them. It is
here, then, that his insistence upon the relationship between
"things-as-they-are and the reality of the imagination" refers itself to the problem of belief. Together they form the

"total reality." Ideals as well as an awareness of "things-as-they-are" can, or should, be kept before us through the agency of the imagination.

To deny freedom to the imagination is to deny a part of the total reality. In an untitled poem in *Notes toward a Supreme Fiction*, Stevens is saying, as he has said in "The Noble Rider and the Sound of Words," that the imagination is adding nothing to human nature that is not inherent in it.

> The freshness of transformation is
> The freshness of a world. It is our own,
> It is ourselves, the freshness of ourselves,
> And that necessity and that presentation
>
> And rubbings of a glass in which we peer.
> Of these beginnings, gay and green, propose
> The suitable amours. Time will write them down.

To deny the imagination is to deny half of what we are. In "Poem with Rhythms," from *Parts of a World*, he further justifies the creations of the imagination. To the metaphor, first stated, of the hand between the candle and the wall, he adds:

> It must be that the hand
> Has a will to grow larger on the wall,
> To grow larger and heavier and stronger than
> The wall; and that the mind
> Turns its own figurations and declares,
>
> *"This image, this love, I compose myself*
> *Of these. In these, I come forth outwardly.*
> *In these, I wear a vital cleanliness,*
> *Not as in air, bright-blue-resembling air,*
> *But as in the powerful mirror of my wish and will."*

Stevens' sense of irony is too keen to allow of his suggesting that the poet be the prophet of a new millennium. His proposal is more modest—that we accept the imagination, and therefore its capacity for helping us live, in esthetic and in moral terms, more humanly. If man cannot be divine, he can be *human*.

The imagination, Stevens insists, leaps out from and plays over an actuality the most unimaginative could not deny. And the very fact that his poems are divisible into themes which taken together state many of the basic problems our society inherits would suggest, on the other hand, a kind of reality the most literal-minded intellectual could not deny. An eagerness to express the immediacy of nature is a characteristic of much modern poetry, including many lines by Stevens; but it is the reality of philosophical problems, particularly in his later work, which most interests him. The two realities are complementary. In them modern poetry has recovered some of the strength that was dissipated by the halfhearted illusion of some nineteenth-century poets that imagination could be kept alive by isolating it from unpleasant physical realities and from philosophical realities, which, it was thought, the scientific minded alone had the right to make authentic pronouncements about. For if the imagination is not mutually interdependent with reality it devolves into what we know as fancy.

In discussing a particular figure of speech employed in *Phaedrus*, Stevens explains its relative ineffectiveness by saying that Plato's "imagination does not adhere to what is real." From this instance he is led to a generalization: "The imagination loses vitality as it ceases to adhere to what is real. When it adheres to the unreal and intensifies what is unreal, while its first effect may be extraordinary, that effect is the maximum effect it will ever have." Plato envisioned the immortal soul as a winged horse and charioteer, then proceeded to develop his characterization of the soul in terms of the figure. Our first reaction, Stevens says, is to identify ourselves with the charioteer that we may fly through the heavens. "Then suddenly we remember, it may be, that the soul no longer exists and we droop in our flight and at last settle on solid ground. The figure becomes antiquated and rustic." The imaginative expression that moves out from something we know as real intensifies its reality, whereas that which moves out from something we know as unreal intensifies its unreality. Or, at least, it makes for the uneasy feeling that we are, at best, experiencing a dream-reality.

The first point that suggests itself relates to the elusive term *reality*. If love, for example, is accepted not as a spiritual reality but only as a delusion the senses exact, then any imaginative extension must be seen merely as intensification of an unreality. Again, if the ideal of nobility is held to be unreal, then the most imaginative statements can not make it real. In other words, the projections, in the forms of ideals and values, of the subjective world must be seen as real before the imagination is free to enlarge upon or to sustain them. Again, as with the style a culture allows itself to create, the agency, imagination, helping to create and sustain ideals and values, must not be merely tolerated or deplored as the human spirit's capacity to create illusions. If it is, then our constant bemoaning that we have been unable to reinstate values as universal factors in reality will be as self-contradictory as one bemoaning his inability to talk after he has torn out his own tongue.

To read Stevens with enjoyment and understanding it is necessary to preceive that each subject, however commonplace or esoteric, becomes a variation upon the all-controlling theme: the role of the human imagination. In writing of the "death of Satan," Lenin, a city getting ready for bed, a bowl of peaches, a lion roaring, modern poetry, a sea voyage, love, war, or whatever, the basic theme is always the same. Consequently in the body of Stevens' poetry one lives in a world of related ideas, with infinite variations and subtleties. The world of *Harmonium* has the greatest density, perhaps, the most exquisite and complex inter-dependencies of color, sound, symbol, and theme. The language of the late books, *Parts of a World* or *Transport to Summer*, is simpler, more direct, more abstract. A part of this impression of an increasingly simplified idiom is, however, illusory. The Stevens of "Sunday Morning" believed that we should find in the

> comforts of the sun,
> In pungent fruit and bright, green wings, or else
> In any balm or beauty of the earth,
> Things to be cherished like the thought of heaven . . .

The Stevens of *Esthétique du Mal* believes that

> The greatest poverty is not to live
> In a physical world . . .

In order to live really in a physical world we have to slough off the cliché forms, get rid of the habit of forcing all knowledge into neatly rational patterns and admit the transforming and ennobling power of the imagination. We must create new forms, new metaphors, new myths in order to experience without distortion the world as *idea* and the world as *body*.

> They will get it straight one day at the
>   Sorbonne.
> We shall return at twilight from the lecture
> Pleased that the irrational is rational.

In order to help us understand and feel the world, the poet creates these new forms, new metaphors, and new myths.

In reading Stevens it is helpful to know in advance that he is employing a complex, ever enlarging symbolism, and a dramatis personae. The abstractness of the later poetry is in part in the mind of the reader who fails to preceive the complexity and to feel the weight of meaning borne by the symbols and characters that live in his mythology.

A full examination of this mythology would require a very extensive study of individual images, symbols and figures recurring and growing by accretion from poem to poem over more than forty years. In a study of the symbolism one would find the sun, the moon, the sea, summer, autumn, geographical regions, color, and musical instruments. The sun in all of Stevens' poetry is the life force, physical existence, the unthinking source. To the sun and all that it symbolizes Stevens opposes "radiant reason" and "radiant will." The moon, the color blue, and musical instruments are constant symbols of the imagination.

> Things as they are
> Are changed upon the blue guitar.

The world sustained by the sun and made beautiful by the moon must be seen in its changing sad and comic colors. Sometimes all these symbols are brought together as in "Credences of Summer."

> The personae of summer play the characters
> Of an inhuman author, who meditates
> With the gold bugs, in blue meadows, late at night.
> He does not hear his characters talk. He sees
> Them mottled, in the moodiest costumes,
>
> Of blue and yellow, sky and sun, belted
> And knotted, sashed and seamed, half pales of red,
> Half pales of green, appropriate habit for

The huge decorum, the manner of the time,
Part of the mottled mood of summer's whole . . .

The dramatis personae, of course, are the human types
who live among the "many blue phenomena" or who attempt to live solely with ideas. Among these characters are
the ascetic, who attempts to see the sky without the blue;
the poet, who helps us design and dominate the world; the
musician or the singer, who like the poet *makes* and for the
moment at least *controls* his world; the hero, who owes his
existence to the willingness of people to conceive and respect heroism; the captain, who acts; the ephebi, who are
the young requiring instruction; the Spaniard, who symbolizes the dark power of the imagination to give character to an
entire people; the valet-comedian, who is the ironic, free intelligence; the puritan townspeople, who do not know the
joys either of exuberance or imagination; the revolutionary,
who is the fanatic ruled by a single "idea In a world of
ideas"; the woman as summer, who is love, fecundity, and
quite apart from sheer rationality; and the rationalist, who
sees the whole truth in limited systems. The rationalists,
like the revolutionists,

                              confine themselves
          To right-angle triangles.
          If they tried rhomboids,
          Cones, wavering lines, ellipses—
          As, for example, the ellipse of the halfmoon—
          Rationalists would wear sombreros.

The rationalist and the revolutionary are examined, as are
all the other figures in Stevens' mythology, against his constant awareness of the nature and function of imagination.
     To examine Stevens' language adequately in order to
place his work requires a fairly detailed study of his most

persistent themes. No such examination can be very successful unless the examiner, knowing in detail the symbols of Stevens' mythology, appreciates and can give a sense of the accurate understanding and practiced ease behind Stevens' ability to separate incredible from credible imaginings and to state the latter so precisely that we seem to see an aspect of reality proliferate and grow luminous before us.

III

The Plays

THE TWO plays are difficult to classify. If the masque must be thought of as theatrical first, with the emphasis primarily upon spectacle and costume, and as literary second, then neither *Three Travellers Watch a Sunrise*[1] nor *Carlos among the Candles*[2] is a masque. The first has singing and brilliant costume, but no dancing. The second has a brilliant costume and a dance, but no music. The theme in each, presented through a central symbolic action, is primary, the spectacle and costume secondary. On the other hand, if complexity of character or a considerable degree of individuality of character is requisite in drama, then neither is a drama.

Apparently the judges for *Poetry* who selected *Three Travellers Watch a Sunrise* as the best among a hundred poetic plays submitted in a contest found it difficult to classify. They were not at all certain of its "dramatic value" but quite sure of its "extraordinary poetic beauty" and its presenting "symbolically a profound truth." When the play was produced by the Provincetown Players in New York, in 1920, the theater critics ignored it. They had not ig-

[1] *Poetry*, VIII (July, 1916), 163–79.
[2] *Poetry*, XI (Dec., 1917), 115–23.

nored *Carlos among the Candles,* produced in New York in
1917. The critic for the *New York Times,* for example,
found it "a baffling monologue . . . intended neither for the
stage nor the library." Quite possibly, as some of the judges
for *Poetry* suspected in reading the earlier play, Stevens'
effects are far too subtle for most audiences. That the plays
have considerable literary merit, however, should be evident to anyone who reads them attentively. And they, like
his prose work, are closely related to the themes and the
points of view expressed in his poetry. It is unfortunate that
neither has been reprinted in any of his volumes.

The dramatis personae of *Three Travellers Watch a
Sunrise* are three Chinese (who may represent wisdom)
and two Negroes (who may represent suffering humanity),
and an Italian girl named Anna, whose lover has hanged
himself. The three Chinese talk, mostly about art. The
Second Chinese, "a man of sense and sympathy," in effect,
makes the point that is to be both dramatized and stated.
There may be beauty in an art created "in seclusion," but
it will have "neither love nor wisdom." These come

> through poverty
> And wretchedness,
> Through suffering and pity.
> It is the invasion of humanity
> That counts.

The porcelain bottle, an art object the Chinese have brought
with them, may call forth wonder, but in finding three dead
men painted thereon one would

> forget the porcelain
> For the figures painted on it.

The Second Chinese is critical of the seclusion of a particular court because it

> woke
> On its windless pavilions,
> And gazed on chosen mornings,
> As it gazed
> On chosen porcelain.

Another recurrent illustration is "the seclusion of sunrise before it shines on any house." The sun "shines, perhaps, for the beauty of shining." But in shining on the earth

> It does not shine on a thing that remains
> What it was yesterday.

Nothing is beautiful except with reference to ourselves and in reference to the knowledge we have, and the experiences we have had.

At about the point in the play when all this becomes clear, the body of Anna's lover is discovered, in the morning light, hanging in a tree. Anna, too, is discovered, numb from terror and grief. When she recovers her senses she tells the Chinese and the Negroes how, because her father had refused to accept him, her lover had hanged himself in front of her.

When the stage is emptied except for himself, the Third Chinese, who has previously favored an impersonal art, perceives a new quality and a new meaning in the redness of the morning sun. For all of them who have witnessed the tragedy, the redness means violence:

> Red is not only
> The color of blood
> Or [Indicating the body]
> Of a man's eyes
> Or [Pointedly]
> Of a girl's. . . .

> Sunrise is multiplied
> Like the earth on which it shines,
> By the eyes that open on it,
> Even dead eyes,
> As red is multiplied by the leaves of the trees.

Carlos among the Candles is a treatment both through the symbolic action and the statements made by Carlos of two themes recurrent in Stevens' work: the influences worked upon us by our environment and our capacity, though limited, to control it. Carlos, the only character in the play, is described as "an eccentric pedant of about forty," dressed in "close fitting breeches and a close fitting tightly buttoned, short coat with long tails," and holding a white lighted taper "high above his head as he moves, fantastically, over the stage, examining the room in which he finds himself." (For the conception of Carlos, Stevens would seem to be in debt to certain nineteenth-century esthetic movements.) On each of the long, low tables on either side of the room are a number of thin black candles.

Carlos is an esthete who ponders the subtle effects upon us of changes made in our surroundings. The candles which he lights and snuffs out, commenting meanwhile in a poetic prose, furnish him with telling examples.

A single candle causes him to be a part of the solitude that fills the room and suggests that he, a small light in the darkness, is incalculable. Two candles dissolve a part of the solitude yet are a little cold, suggesting a respectable company, whereas three suggest that people are about to gather and that the room itself will be forgotten. Four candles seem a luxury, five change luxury to magnificence, six are the beginning of splendor. Having made these and other observations, he decides that six candles, having enabled him to live imaginatively under many and varied conditions, "burn like an adventure that has been completed."

Then he lights another and another, his spirits rising constantly, until he has lighted twelve.

Turning to the second table, he is reminded of darkness. "Darkness expels me." After drawing aside the curtain to the window, he lights each of the second twelve. The light is so great that it falls on the flowers outside the window. Now the darkness and the semidarkness are expelled. It is in such light that an exquisite human world is possible.

> Here there will be silks and fans . . . the
> movement of arms . . . rumors of Renoir . . .
> coiffures . . . hands . . . scorn of Debussy . . .
> communications of body to body. . . . There
> will be servants, as fat as plums, bearing
> pineapples from the Azores. . . .

Then a gust of night wind blows out several of the candles. Carlos *"buries his head in his arms. . . . In a burst of feeling, he blows out all the candles that are still burning on the table at the left."* The remaining candles furnish him, as he blows them out one by one, with a series of melancholy metaphors, among them these:

> What is there in the extinguishing of light?
> It is like twelve birds flying in autumn.
>
> It is like three peregrins, departing
>
> The extinguishing of light is like that old
>   Hesper,
> Clapped upon the clouds.

There is, finally, a single spot where the star *was* bright in the sky—then it is merely a memory. Having finished his little game among the candles, Carlos goes to the window

once more. He studies the darkness. Then, before spring-
ing through the window, he speaks with elation:

Oh, ho! Here is a matter beyond invention.

That this play, an expanded metaphor, is recognizably
of a piece with his later work becomes evident in reading
the concluding lines of *Esthétique du Mal*:

And out of what one sees and hears and out
Of what one feels, who could have thought to make
So many selves, so many sensuous worlds,
As if the air, the mid-day air, was swarming
With the metaphysical changes that occur,
Merely in living as and where we live.

Stevens as a poet is an explicator. His subject is esthetics,
not merely in its relation to sensibility and intellect but to
belief, morality, and society. Of the two plays, one may
guess, only *Carlos among the Candles* might be effective in
the theater. And its interest would be as choreography and
as the statement of a theme. Neither play satisfies the usual
demand for entertainment to be found in action itself or in
the stress or changes caused in a group of characters by the
action. Many plays serve as "entertainment" for audiences
not interested, at least primarily, in their thematic statement. The primary emphasis, the *sine qua non*, of Stevens'
plays is theme. They may be characterized, providing the
term is not used as a pejorative, as closet dramas. It may
well be that the writing of these plays convinced Stevens
that his talent is philosophical, expository, and narrative
rather than dramatic. If there is a characteristic persistent
throughout Stevens' work, it is his impersonality. There are
in discussions of other writers no little personal asides. He
gives no attention to the fullness of their personalities. It is

also true that there are no *people,* there are merely generally symbolic figures, in his poems or in his plays. There
are only ideas about people and aspects of people. There is,
on the other hand, a constant process of abstraction that
serves his theory of poetry. As one looks back over the
range of his work it becomes evident that Stevens' interests
have always been in the direction of theory. His advice to
William Carlos Williams in 1917 was that the poet needs
a focus and a central point of reference. Instead of shifting
and changing points of view the poet holding to a single
focus would enlarge and qualify his understanding of his
subject. Stevens in holding over the years to his subject has
enlarged his understanding of the nature of poetry and the
implications of its enormous role.

IV

The Prose

Stevens is not usually thought of as a critic. Considering the limited amount of prose he has written and the closely restricted nature of the subjects he has treated, perhaps he should not be regarded as a critic. It is also true that his criticism has always been neatly related to his own problems as a poet.

On the other hand, he has written some very important criticism, in his poetry as well as in his prose. In more recent years especially his work has become an important formative influence on younger poets. Also it is fairly clear, as witness Eliot's comments in his lecture (1947) on Milton, that most of the poet-critics have written their criticism out of their own problems as poets. Lastly, the poetry as well as the prose he has written in the past ten or fifteen years makes it unmistakably clear that Stevens' interests have become increasingly critical.

He himself has said, "There is nothing that I desire more intensely than to make a contribution to the theory of poetry." At the same time, however, he knows that the prose he has written—brief comments on his own poems; comments on or reviews of the work of other poets; public lectures; answers to questionnaires, and jottings on the na-

ture and problems of poetry—could not, except in Procrus-
tean fashion, be drawn taut and tied together in a coherent
volume on the theory of poetry. Nonetheless, the prose is
eminently worthy of some study, both for the theory it does
set forth and as a way into Stevens' own poetry. Perhaps it
can be examined most easily if it is treated, somewhat arbi-
trarily, in the four categories just mentioned.

Comments on his own poetry. William Carlos Williams
published a letter from Stevens, written after the publication of *Al Que Quiere* (1917), which indicates that from
the very beginning of his career Stevens has striven to work
within a given subject and to develop his techniques in
terms of it.[1]

> Personally I have a distaste for miscellany. . . . Given a
> fixed point of view, realistic, imagistic, or what you will,
> everything adjusts itself to that point of view; and the proc-
> ess of adjustment is a world of flux, as it should be for the
> poet. But to fidget with points of view leads always to new
> beginnings and incessant new beginnings lead to sterility.
> A single manner or mood thoroughly matured and exploited
> is that fresh thing. . . . I am only objecting that a book that
> contains your particular quality should contain anything
> else and suggesting that if the quality were carried to a
> communicable extreme, in intensity and volume, etc. . . .
> I return Pound's letter. Observe how in everything he does
> he proceeds with the greatest positiveness. . . .

Possibly no other poet with abilities comparable to Stevens'
has worked so intensively and extensively with the same
subject—the relations of imagination and reality—over so
many years. It is interesting, whether one agrees with the
procedure, to know that this has always been his intention.

[1] See *Kora in Hell* by William Carlos Williams (Boston, The Four
Seas Company, 1920), pp. 17–18.

On at least three occasions Stevens has contributed notes to anthologies in which his own poems have appeared.[2] For Mr. Benét's *Fifty Poets* Stevens selected "The Emperor of Ice Cream" as his favorite poem on these grounds:

> This wears a deliberately commonplace costume, and yet seems to me to contain something of the essential gaudiness of poetry; that is the reason why I like it. . . . I dislike niggling, and like letting myself go. Poems of this sort are the pleasantest on which to look back, because they seem to remain fresher than others.

His use of the term "gaudiness" implies perhaps that Stevens was concerned with two aspects of poetry: brilliant or highly colored details, and a free but reined imagination. But for Mr. Burnett's *This Is My Best* Stevens selected as his best poem "Domination of Black." The nature of the note he wrote for this volume suggests that Stevens was concerned less with explaining why he selected this poem than with stating that poetry should be accepted *as* poetry and not as politics or philosophy.

> Poetry is poetry, and one's objective as a poet is to achieve poetry, precisely as one's objective in music is to achieve music. There are poets who would regard that as a scandal and who would say that a poem that had no importance except its importance as poetry had no importance at all, and that a poet who had no objective except to achieve poetry was a fribble and something less than a man of reason.

This is a subject to which he returns again and again, in his poetry as well as in his prose. In the note he did for the *Oxford Anthology of American Literature* Stevens repeated that his intention was to write poetry, not something else

[2] In *Fifty Poets*, ed. W. R. Benét (New York, Duffield and Green, 1933), p. 46; in *Oxford Anthology of American Literature*, eds. W. R. Benét and N. H. Pearson (New York, Oxford University Press, 1936), p. 1325; and in *This Is My Best*, ed. Whit Burnett (New York, The Dial Press, 1942), p. 652.

under the guise of poetry, simply "because I feel the need
of doing it." To this remark he adds a statement about
form: "The essential thing in form is to be free in whatever form is used. A free form does not assure freedom."
The cult of undisciplined freedom destroyed many poets in
Stevens' generation. They knew, as someone has put it,
what free verse was free *from*, but, unlike Stevens, not
what it was free *for*. He believes, in other words, in those
forms that make freedom inside them possible.

There is also a note which he did for the jacket of *The
Man With the Blue Guitar & Other Poems*, a volume in
which, of course, *Owl's Clover* was reprinted. He wrote
that although *Owl's Clover* reflected the political furor of
the thirties his intention had been to point up the opposition "between things as they are and things imagined; in
short, to isolate poetry." He added that the poems in *The
Man With the Blue Guitar* were written as a result of
thinking about the problem of poetry in a period of great
changes:

> I have been making notes on the subject in the form of
> short poems during the past winter. These short poems,
> some thirty of them, form the other group, "The Man With
> the Blue Guitar," from which the book takes its title. This
> group deals with the incessant conjunctioning between
> things as they are and things imagined. Although the blue
> guitar is a symbol of the imagination, it is used most often
> simply as a reference to the individuality of the poet, mean-
> ing by the poet any man of imagination.

It is true that the subject is treated most explicitly in this
volume, but it is equally true that it is treated, even though
indirectly, in all of his poetry and prose.

Comments on the work of other writers. Stevens has written reviews, articles or notes about a number of his con-

temporaries: William Carlos Williams, Eliot, Marianne Moore, Paul Rosenfeld, and John Crowe Ransom. About Williams he has written, if one includes the letter reprinted in *Kora in Hell*, three times; about Miss Moore he has written twice. Stevens wrote an introduction, or preface, for Williams' *Collected Poems: 1921–1931* [3] which has been used apparently by a majority of the critics who have written about Williams. He put his finger on the central characteristic of Williams, a tendency toward sentimentality held in check by a "passion for the anti-poetic. . . . The anti-poetic is his spirit's cure. He needs it as a naked man needs shelter or as an animal needs salt." Quite naturally Stevens has always refused to accept the connotations that the terms *romantic* and *realist* usually hold in our time. In his comments on Williams' poems he gives by implication his reasons:

> Something of the unreal is necessary to fecundate the real; something of the sentimental is necessary to fecundate the anti-poetic. Williams, by nature, is more of a realist than is commonly true in the case of a poet. . . . [A]nd generally speaking one might run through these pages and point out how often the essential poetry is the result of the conjunction of the unreal and the real, the sentimental and the anti-poetic, the constant interaction of two opposites.

The romantic poet today—and Williams is one—Stevens continues, "is the hermit who dwells alone with the sun and moon, but insists on taking a rotten newspaper."

About Eliot, Stevens has written very little, but that little indicates his great respect for him: [4]

> At one time or another I have been under some great teachers but I have had only two Masters, and one of them is T. S. Eliot. My personal acquaintance with Eliot has

[3] New York, Objectivist Press, 1934, pp. 1–4.
[4] See *The Harvard Advocate*, CXXV (Dec., 1938), 41–42.

been slight, being confined chiefly to correspondence; yet
for about sixteen years I have been trying to learn everything from him that I can use.

In his review of Miss Moore's *Selected Poems,* Stevens re-
marks that Eliot is the "most brilliant instance" today of a
poet who can make the romantic seem genuine and living.
The chief lesson that Eliot had to give to his contemporaries, Stevens added, is this: "If poetry is an art greater
than the poet, then great labor, restraint, and constant self-
effacement from the work are all necessary if we are to contribute anything of value to that art."

The closest examination of a fellow writer Stevens has
done is his review, "A Poet that Matters," [5] of Marianne
Moore's *Selected Poems.* It is an intensive examination of
the sort one expects from a critic like Cleanth Brooks. (It is
possible despite their obvious differences that Miss Moore
and Stevens have more in common as poets than either has
with any other contemporary.) He explains the structure
of her verses, her use of half-rhymes, the variations in the
strength of sounds, and so forth. He also discusses her characteristic "hybridization," as he calls it, of the real and the
romantic. "Moon-vines are moon-vines and tedious. But
moon-vines trained on fishing twine are something else and
they are as perfectly as it is possible for anything to be what
interests Miss Moore." Stevens quotes other lines in his attempt to show that "romantic" should, among its various
meanings, include the sense of "living." "It is absurd to
wince at being called a romantic poet. Unless one is that,
one is not a poet at all." But the romantic poet, as he said
in connection with Williams and will repeat again and
again, must also be intelligent, know what is genuine and
what is not. The poet needs wit as well as probity. Stevens
is getting closer to the position he will ultimately attempt

[5] *Life and Letters Today,* XIII (Dec., 1935), 61–65.

to state in his lectures. His examinations of Williams and
Miss Moore undoubtedly helped him to clarify it, but it is
interesting to note that he was not quite ready to make necessary distinctions when he wrote:

> The romantic that falsifies is rot and that is true even though
> the romantic inevitably falsifies: it falsifies but it does not
> vitiate. It is an association of the true and the false. It is
> not the true. It is not the false. It is both. The school of
> poetry that believes in sticking to the facts would be stoned
> if it was not sticking to the facts in a world in which there
> are no facts: or some such thing.

The "some such thing" becomes clearer in the later prose
of Stevens.

The most recent of Stevens' comments on Williams is
his "Rubbings of Reality," done for the William Carlos
Williams Issue of the *Briarcliff Quarterly*.[6] He presents
Williams, this time, as a poet who is "merely practicing to
make perfect," who practices to get at his subject. He goes
on to say, also, that in a world re-made according to the
lights of our intelligence Williams' poems would have a
place. He seems to be hinting, however, that Williams has
never quite managed to get into a subject, at least a big,
interrelated subject. "Is not Williams in a sense a literary
pietist, chastening himself incessantly, along the Passaic?"

Stevens' contribution, entitled "The Shaper," to the
memorial volume, *Paul Rosenfeld: Voyager in the Arts*,[7] is
somewhat similar to the piece on Williams. Neither is a detailed investigation of the interrelated characteristics of a
writer's work. Each, on the contrary, is concerned with a
single characteristic which, true enough of the specific
writer, might also be true of other writers. This same com-

[6] III (Oct., 1946), 201–202.
[7] Eds. Jerome Mellquist and Lucie Wiese (New York, Creative Age
Press, 1949), pp. 98–100.

ment might be made about his "John Crowe Ransom: Tennessean,"[8] contributed to the "Homage to John Crowe Ransom" symposium. Stevens presents Rosenfeld as a man who was more concerned with helping the writers of his generation find means of becoming choate than with isolating himself and finding the means necessary if he himself was to bring one of the arts to a high degree of discipline and form. He has nothing specific to say about the writings of Rosenfeld, just as he has almost nothing to say, in the more recent essay, about the specific nature of Williams' poetry. Rosenfeld is a *"Schopfer,"* whose art is human relations; Williams is an instinctive writer, a practicer getting ready for a subject.

The little essay on Ransom may be Stevens at his best in writing prose. There is a delusive simplicity in his saying that Ransom's distinction is in his capacity to make a legend of reality. He implies a number of things, and his account of what he means certainly makes the gifts of Ransom the poet much more understandable. But, one must add, with certain changes in geography what he says might be read as a good account of Yeats. He sees Ransom as a Tennessean who knows and loves his country intimately, as an insider knows and loves it. But he is also the outsider, the artist, who can see it in "its precise line and look," and who can make a legend, but not a vulgarized legend, of it. He does not idealize, caricature, or add trimmings to what *is;* the Tennessee of Ransom's poems and legend is no "pastiche." He can make commonplace things reveal themselves by the expedient of catching them in his imagination and making them a part of the "peculiar legend of things as they are when they are as we want them to be."

In his long note on Marianne Moore, contributed to the issue of the *Quarterly Review of Literature*[9] devoted to an

[8] *The Sewanee Review,* LVI (Summer, 1948), 367–69.
[9] IV (1948), 143–49.

examination of her work Stevens is concerned with the need for the poet who can perceive and state "a reality adequate to the profound necessities of life today or for that matter any day." Every age that is not to become "decadent or barbarous," Stevens says, must have a sense that certain things are real and solid, "the sense that we can touch and feel a solid reality which does not wholly dissolve itself into the conceptions of our own minds." The sense that certain things are real and can be depended on as points of reference and belief makes for a sense of security and sanity. No individual fact offers such a security. There must be a pattern of facts that we accept as real. Miss Moore, for example, with her profound sense of what is genuine and what is presumptuous presents in such a poem as "He 'Digesteth Harde Yron'" a sense of the moral order that makes for security. "The gist of the poem is that the camel-sparrow has escaped the greed that has led to the extinction of other birds linked to it in size by its solicitude for its own welfare and that of its chicks." The poet deals with an "individual reality," as in the poem Stevens discusses, and if the insight is sharp and the presentation successful the reader is free to achieve a realization of an important aspect of reality. The "saying" of a poem and the way it is said can furnish a "revelation of reality." Miss Moore, he continues, is a valuable poet in our time because she is humble, one of those "that move about the world with the lure of the real in their hearts." She is among those who can see through fallacious and empty forms; "she has the faculty of digesting the 'harde yron' of appearance." By giving us a sense of reality, by mediating "for us a reality not ourselves" she furnishes us with necessary knowledge, thereby, as Stevens has said in another essay, helping us to live our lives. In his earlier piece on Miss Moore, Stevens was not quite ready or able to say that her kind of "romanticism" was either "true" or "false." In this later commentary, by

stating the problem in terms of "appearance" and "reality,"
he avoids to some extent the sense of unreality we, as contemporaries, have in using the term "romanticism."

Lectures. Five of Stevens' six lectures on poetry have been
published. The sixth, the unpublished lecture, was delivered at Harvard some years ago. The lecture which has received most attention is "The Noble Rider and the Sound
of Words," one of the Mesures lectures at Princeton, published in *The Language of Poetry*.[10] This is the fullest and
clearest exposition of Stevens' theory of poetry up to this
time, and it may be, despite a certain amount of padding,
the most illuminating and important of all his prose pieces.
The primary point of the lecture is that a flight of the
imagination in a poem or work of art has strength only in
terms of its being related to what we know as real. A work
of the imagination to be vital must have "the strength of
reality or none at all." Further, some periods have greater
faith in the power of imagination, greater belief in the existence of nobility of character, and are less subject to the
multiple distractions and storms of reality that preclude the
quiet of mind necessary for the workings of the imagination.

> To sum it up, the pressure of reality is, I think, the deter-
> mining character of an era and, as well, the determining
> factor in the artistic character of an individual. The resist-
> ance to this pressure or its evasion in the case of individuals
> of extraordinary imagination cancels the pressure so far as
> these individuals are concerned.

Stevens discusses periods of denotative and connotative expression in terms of the one being "favorable to reality" and
the other to imagination. But he is not primarily concerned

[10] Ed. Allen Tate (Princeton, N. J., Princeton University Press,
1942), pp. 91–125.

in this lecture with language or metrics—he is concerned with the sources of poetry, and with speculating about the factors in the individual and in the society that are favorable and unfavorable to the writing of it.

"The Figure of the Youth as Virile Poet" [11] is a closely reasoned statement of the nature of poetry, particularly in our time. Stevens in this paper works not so much toward a definition of poetry as toward the circumscribing of an area which must be seen clearly if the nature and function of poetry are to be understood. He says, as a "statement of convenience," that in philosophy we attempt to approach truth through the reason but in poetry we attempt to approach truth through the imagination. We may admire poetry that satisfies the imagination even though it does not satisfy the reason, but we are more deeply satisfied by a poetry that satisfies both. He is saying, as he has said before, that the poet must work with what we accept as credible. Poetry is also personal in that the mind of the poet is constantly describing itself, but the poet creates a world in which the reader may become naturalized and liberated. He creates a *"mundo* of the imagination in which the imaginative man delights and not the gaunt world of reason."* Stevens would dismiss the notion of a "mystic muse," but on the other hand he wants a place for poetry in our conception of the true. Poetry is a part of what is real, even as the poet himself is:

> *I am the truth, since I am part of what is real, but neither more nor less than those around me. And I am imagination, in a leaden time and in a world that does not move for the weight of its own heaviness.*

All of us live to some extent in our sensibilities but the poet-genius "not only accumulates experiences with greater rapidity, but accumulates experiences and qualities of ex-

[11] *Sewanee Review,* LII (Autumn, 1944), 508–29.

perience accessible only in the extreme ranges of sensibility." The philosopher, Stevens says, tends to dwell with reason, the priest with belief, and the poet with imagination. Stevens has no belief in the existence of truth as "a static concept." Yet he holds that the *kind* of truth associated with poetry is dependent both upon poetry's holding close to what we accept as real and upon our being "disposed to be strongly influenced" by the imagination.

Three Academic Pieces, consisting of a lecture entitled "The Realm of Resemblance" and two poems, "Someone Puts a Pineapple Together" and "Of Ideal Time and Choice," was read at Harvard, published in *Partisan Review* and then republished by the Cummington Press.[12] It is an interesting example of the way Stevens has in recent years written about the same subject, the theory of poetry, both in his poetry and in his prose. And it is interesting in that it exemplifies the greater assurance with which Stevens employs the terminology of his own criticism. In "The Realm of Resemblance" he no longer says, as he did say, at least by implication, in his review of Miss Moore's *Selected Poems,* that in the language of genuine poetry the true and the false are closely associated. He no longer feels a need to use such a pejorative as "false" in discussing the metaphors of the poet:

> We have been trying to get at a truth about poetry, to get at one of the principles that compose the theory of poetry. It comes to this, that poetry is a part of the structure of reality. If this has been demonstrated, it pretty much amounts to saying that the structure of poetry and the structure of reality are one or, in effect, that poetry and reality are one, or should be.

He no longer hesitates to deplore or to ridicule the consequences of reductive naturalism that tend to deny the

[12] Cummington, Mass., 1947.

human imagination and the reality of the moral and esthetic realms it enables us to create and to live with. "One may find intimations of immortality in an object on the mantelpiece; and the intimations are as real in the mind in which they occur as the mantelpiece itself."

Stevens does not, by and large, lean on any of the bodies of documentation that exist for the subjects he treats. He writes as a practitioner who knows about the problems and nature of poetry at first hand. Nor does he write at length. Consequently, as in "The Realm of Resemblance," one finds generalized statements like the following:

> Poetry is a satisfying of the desire for resemblance. As the mere satisfying of a desire, it is pleasurable. But poetry if it did nothing but satisfy a desire would not rise above the level of many lesser things. Its singularity is that in the act of satisfying the desire for resemblance it touches the sense of reality, heightens it, intensifies it. If resemblance is described as a partial similarity between two dissimilar things, it complements and reinforces that which the two dissimilar things have in common. It makes it brilliant.

This might do as a beginning, particularly if other aspects of poetry relating to it were developed at length, but they are as likely as not to be touched on merely in a single sentence, as in the statements: "Perhaps the whole field of connotation is based on resemblance." "The ambiguity that is so favorable to the poetic mind is precisely the ambiguity favorable to resemblance," and "the desire to enjoy reality . . . is the desire for elegance." If a subject such as this were treated in detail and with the insight Stevens is capable of we would undoubtedly have an important addition to the theory of poetry. We should, however, be grateful for what he has written, generalized essays and lectures quickened by many brilliant *aperçus*.

"Effects of Analogy" was delivered as one of the Bergen

Lectures at Yale University and later published in the *Yale Review*.[13] This lecture, like "The Realm of Resemblance," has a few germinal and provocative statements, none of which is developed in any detail. Stevens analyzes a few images and analogies with considerable perception, concluding that a given analogy is significant or meaningful only when a part, a particular, of an image is elaborated.

In the lines from Leonidas, "Even as a vine on her dry pole I support myself now on a staff and Death calls me to Hades," the particular is the staff. This becomes the dry pole and the vine follows after. There is no analogy between a vine and an old man in all circumstances. But when one supports itself on a dry pole and the other on a staff the case is different.

Secondly, he notes, "every image is a restatement of the subject of the image in terms of an attitude." These observations are also related to such subjects as the individual poet's need for having his own subject, the belief (with which Stevens disagrees) that "ivory tower" writing is necessarily weak, the relation of the poet to his community, the contemporary sense of what is musical in poetic language, and so forth. The lecture is mildly provocative, but it seems to promise more than it gives. The choice of the subject, the nature of analogies, may suggest how much Stevens at this point in his career is interested in the theory of poetic language.

"Imagination as Value," delivered as a lecture at the English Institute,[14] repeats a number of points Stevens has made elsewhere, about the "romantic" falsifying when it denies the real, about the need to see imagination not as the logical positivists see it but as a "clue to reality," and about its service in the economy of human affairs, that is,

[13] XXXVIII (Sept., 1948), 29–44.
[14] *English Institute Annual,* 1949.

in social and political realms as well as in the arts. Stevens is concerned that imagination be studied not only as it manifests itself in arts and letters but in political, social and other cultural forms. No longer, for the most part, do we place rationality in direct opposition to imagination. Artifice is not necessarily a pejorative term for Stevens:

> If when the primacy of the intelligence has been achieved, one can really say what a man is actually like, what could be more natural than a science of illusions? Moreover, if the imagination is not quite the clue to reality now, might it not become so then? As for the present, what have we, if we do not have science, except the imagination? And who is to say of its deliberate fictions arising out of the contemporary mind that they are not forerunners of some such science? There is more than the romantic in the statement that the true work of art, whatever it may be, is not the work of the individual artist. It is time and it is place, as these perfect themselves.

To realize these matters adequately "is to realize the extent of artifice."

Prose jottings and answers to questionnaires. The remaining prose pieces written by Stevens are two brief series of epigrammatic jottings about poetry, the sort of thing many poets set down in their journals, called "Materia Poetica," [15] a note on war poetry, printed as an appendix to his *Parts of a World*,[16] and answers to three questionnaires, one for the British *Twentieth Century Verse*,[17] and two for *Partisan Review*.[18]

Many of the statements in "Materia Poetica" are similar to statements, usually much expanded, which appear in the

[15] *View*, I (Sept., 1940), 3, and II (Oct., 1942), 28.
[16] New York, Alfred A. Knopf, 1942.
[17] XII–XIII (Oct., 1938), 107 and 112.
[18] VI (Summer, 1939), 39–40; and XV (Aug., 1948), 884–86.

essays and lectures, or even in his poetry. Thus, for example, we find: "A dead romantic is a falsification," or "In
poetry, at least, the imagination must not detach itself from
reality." Again, "Poetry increases the feeling for reality."
Many of these thirty-nine jottings are burgeoning with implications, not a few of which could be discovered by examining Stevens' own practice as a poet. Thus the dictum:
"Accuracy of observation is the equivalent of accuracy of
thinking." Somewhat similarly, his criticism of surrealism
implies his view as a poet of the way *in* to a subject:

> The essential fault of surrealism is that it invents without
> discovering. To make a clam play an accordion is to invent,
> not to discover. The observation of the unconscious, so far
> as it can be observed, should reveal things of which we
> have previously been unconscious, not the familiar things of
> which we have been conscious plus imagination.

The note on war poetry, in part, is an expansion of one
of the statements in "Materia Poetica": "Collecting poetry
from one's experience as one goes along is not the same
thing as merely writing poetry." Certain events, such as
"the violent reality of war," fill the consciousness and dominate it. Thus the phenomenon in war time of certain people's writing poetry, as a release from their consciousness
of tremendous and sometimes heroic events, who will write
very little poetry in peacetime for the simple reason that
their imaginations do not press in on them, urging them to
write. Such writing is in some fashion a coming to terms
with fact. It goes on although to a lesser extent in peacetime as well. "The poetry of a work of the imagination constantly illustrates the fundamental and endless struggle
with fact." And it will continue to go on. "Nothing will
ever appease this desire except a consciousness of fact as
everyone is at least satisfied to have it be." This brief

note, only a page in length, is indicative of much of Stevens' prose. It states a point briefly, then merely adds an aside or two. One would like him to go on, to follow up the implications of his point, to illustrate it, and to say, for example, what it means for poetry in various periods. Even so, the point is germinal and an invitation to further thought.

Stevens' answers to the questionnaire, "Enquiry About American Poetry," touch on two or three points that suggest his awareness of the period he has lived in and people he has written among. He believes there is now "a clear sense of what is American" (which should be evident, say, to an Englishman reading our poetry) despite the fact that we "are a bit tentative racially." He says, however, that the fact that we are not as yet racially assimilated to any considerable extent prevents our having much in the way of a tradition. Again, just what he means by tradition is not followed up. What is it that Americans have "in common" and which gives them an "American character" but at the same time is not from a "tradition"?

Stevens' replies to the second of the *Partisan Review* questionnaires raises at least two problems he has been concerned with elsewhere: the relation between poetry and politics, and the place of poetry in our time. In this more recent comment for *Partisan Review* he repeats that the poet must remain clear on one point:

> In the conflict between the poet and the politician the chief honor the poet can hope for is that of remaining himself. Life and reality, on the one hand, and politics, on the other, notwithstanding the activity of politics, are not interchangeable terms.

In his comment on the place of poetry in our time he repeats a notion that recurs in his later work. In "Materia Poetica" he had said:

The relation of art to life is of the first importance especially in a skeptical age since, in the absence of a belief in God, the mind turns to its own creations and examines them, not alone from the aesthetic point of view, but for what they reveal, for what they validate and invalidate, for the support they give.

Progressively he has come to believe in the basic and fundamental importance of poetry in our time as a way of furnishing us with a view of the world. He now believes

> that poetic order is potentially as significant as philosophical order. Accordingly, it is natural to project the idea of a theory of poetry that would be pretty much the same thing as a theory of the world based on a coordination of the poetic aspects of the world. Such an idea completely changes the significance of poetry. It does what poetry itself does, that is to say, it leads to a fresh conception of the world. . . . Many sensitive readers of poetry, without being mystics or romantics or metaphysicians, feel that there probably is available in reality something accessible through a theory of poetry which would make a profound difference in our sense of the world.

Stevens, one cannot help believing, is among those who believe that this may be so.

V

The Politics of Order

THE POETRY of Wallace Stevens, particularly during the thirties, has been attacked from the left. Stanley Burnshaw, in *The New Masses*, Oct. 1, 1935, found a "strange confusion" in *Ideas of Order.* The earlier work of Stevens, he said, was of a kind "that people concerned with the murderous world collapse can hardly swallow today except in tiny doses." If Stevens was to develop into a valuable poet for his time he would have to "sweep his contradictory notions into a valid Idea of Order."

That Stevens and his critic had different notions about *valid* ideas of order became even more clearly apparent when he wrote *Owl's Clover*. Parts of this poem appeared first under the title "Mr. Burnshaw and the Statue," in *The New Caravan*, for 1936. The poem is not so much an answer to Mr. Burnshaw as an extension of the themes treated earlier. But, as Stevens himself wrote, *Owl's Clover*, while emphasizing "the opposition between things as they are and things imagined," does "reflect what was then going on in the world." Nor did he ignore the issue, the "necessity" for a world order, developing out of a detailed and exact set of political blueprints, as Burnshaw stated it. "The Old Woman and the Statue" which appeared in

the *Southern Review,* Summer, 1935, continues the investigation of themes treated in *Ideas of Order.* It was to be
the first section of the longest poem Stevens has written—
Owl's Clover. Some months later the second edition, "Mr.
Burnshaw and the Statue," appeared. The title would suggest that this was a reply to Mr. Burnshaw's strictures in
his *New Masses* review. Despite the references to Mr.
Burnshaw, which were dropped in the later version of
Owl's Clover,[1] the second section is a continuation, holding
to the symbol of the statue, of the earlier poem. The remaining sections, "The Greenest Continent," "A Duck for
Dinner," and "Sombre Figuration," appeared only in book
form. In the revised version of *Owl's Clover* there are many
changes, long and short passages dropped and a number of
lines and passages thoroughly rewritten. In *Owl's Clover*
Stevens has written his finest long poem and undoubtedly
one of the best long poems in English published during the
first half of the twentieth century.

Fortunately Stevens found a strong and sufficiently complex symbol to hold his poem together. It serves him as
the symbol of the waste land served Eliot or the symbol
of the Virgin served Henry Adams. The Statue, symbol-
izing an older and now moribund civilization, is the center of the poem. In "The Old Woman and the Statue"
the situation treated is essentially this: "A group of marble
horses," their heads high and their muscles taut, is poised
for a plunge, for a great leap into the air, in some coura-
geous or noble action. The sculptor had conceived them in
some such terms as these. The reader sees them thus one
somber day in autumn. In front of the statue a destitute
old woman appears, but so poverty stricken and so lonely
is she that the statue is meaningless to her: "The mass of

[1] New York, Alcestis Press, 1936. The references were also dropped
in the version published in the volume *The Man With the Blue Guitar
& Other Poems,* 1937.

stone collapsed to marble hulk." In the evening darkness
the night itself becomes "the sovereign shape in a world of
shapes." We might, knowing the night and the wind, have
a need in us to create a symbol of strength and hopeful-
ness. The symbol might be the yew tree, "great and grave
beyond imagined trees." Suffering is temporary even though
the wind and the night signify disturbing and destructive
forces that are actual and permanent. If we were free from
suffering long enough to create and to sustain the yew tree
as symbol, the horses, the statue, would rise again, the legs

> Would flash in air, and the muscular bodies thrust
> Hoofs grinding against the stubborn earth . . .

Because the statue symbolizes the aspirations and the virtues of a world now moribund it seems "a thing from
Schwarz's," an antique. The newer aspirations, we are reminded in "The Statue at the World's End," are concerned
not with the past but with the future, and not so much
with the individual as with men in the mass. This is the
newer dream attempting to find a shape, attempting to in-
form a new society. Stevens apparently accepts the inevitability of this. He and his kind will shed a tear or two and
be a bit nostalgic for the world that created the statue.
There are, we may note, these ironic lines, presented as a
part of his awareness of the change. The buzzards

> eat the bellies of the rich,
> Fat with a thousand butters.

But we should not believe the future will bring the millennium. We will move

> out of the waste of the past
> Into a hopeful waste to come.

And he adds the conservative note that no enormous plans
for a future society can be put into working order suddenly
without violence and destruction. The changes should
evolve. Any world will have its limitations. Those prophe-
sying and ushering in the new one should be candid and
honest. Referring to the statue, he says,

> The stones
> That will replace shall be carved, *"The Mass
> Appoints These Marbles Of Itself To Be
> Itself."* No more than that, no subterfuge,
> No memorable muffing, bare and blunt.

"The Greenest Continent," the third section of the
poem, is quite similar in part to Ruskin's "The Nature of
Gothic" chapter in *Stones of Venice*. The statue, the
marble horses, belongs to a northern world:

> It came
> If not from winter, from a summer like
> A winter's noon, in which the colors sprang
> From snow, and would return again to snow,
> As summer would return to weazened days.

The statue would be inappropriate in Africa where
death, sudden, serpentine, and sinuous, rules the imagination. In other words the gods of the north or the gods that
once were the gods of the north are not the gods of Africa.
Have they, then, nothing in common? They have Ananke,
the forces indifferent to man, who dictates where the statue
will be raised, or not raised, as "the common god." To him
the external forms that rise out of the mind of the north or
the mind of Africa are an indifferent matter. To Ananke,
to whom the verses of poets are the same as litanies, it

makes no difference that the "Heaven of Europe is empty."
Section IV, "A Duck for Dinner," re-examines the dream
of the future in terms of the kind of individualism the
American has known—"As the man the state, not the state
the man." The "abstract man" is a meaningless phrase;
there are only men, formed by the world that has made
them. Our world has been the world of the statue. Turning
from the dream of heaven to the dream of the future will
take "time and tinkering." Changes will come, but they
should come in a way that is

> More of ourselves in a world that is more our own . . . .

The "envoi to the past" was certainly one of the most pre-
posterous planks in the political platform that foretold the
brave new world. Even now, some years after their break
with the "bourgeois past" the Soviets are rediscovering that
certain institutions are human rather than bourgeois.[2] The
future must be in terms of what we are, "more our own."
Knowing ourselves and knowing the past we cannot promise a duck on Sunday to each of a million. We can offer
hope—but we should do well to remember that the future
is likely to be another winding of the clock.

"Sombre Figuration," the final section, picks up and develops an earlier theme, the limitations of the reason. It
may be that

> reason, fatuous fire,
> Is only another egoist wearing a mask . . . .

There is another man, a second self, within us whom Stevens calls the "subman."

[2] See, for example, Alexander Werth, "Marriage in Russia," *The
Nation*, CLXVI (Apr. 24, 1948), 436–37.

The man below
Imagines and it is true, as if he thought
By imagining, anti-logician, quick
With the logic of transforming certitudes.

He has created ages in which people lived as among solid
objects, unalterable laws and manners. But the "cycle of
the solid having turned" we find ourselves painfully aware
of the flux, "the cat-eyed atmosphere." Because we live
with, and in part are, the subman we should suspect the
blueprints for the brave new world: "The future must bear
within it every past." Nonetheless we are "a generation
that does not know itself." It is as though the statue were
in perspective against space itself, and as though seen by
the crow flying, it were all heads, backs and haunches. We
are in a period, readying itself for change, when the imagination is still. Caught between the past and the future we
know a kind of rare passion, rare because of

Night and imagination being one . . . .

At some places in *Owl's Clover* the coming of a quite different, a transformed, world is both foretold and accepted
as inevitable but at other places only modifications, slight
changes are seen as coming. The reason for this may be,
simply enough, that Stevens could see the inevitability of
change but wished in his own little world to see it come
very slowly.

In May, 1937, *Poetry* published 13 of the 33 sections that
would compose "The Man With the Blue Guitar." It was
published the following fall in book form, as *The Man
With the Blue Guitar & Other Poems*. In the same volume
were "Owl's Clover," "A Thought Revolved," and "The

Men That Are Falling," which had won *The Nation's* poetry prize the preceding year. The poems, done in irregular and for the most part unrhymed couplets, are, as Stevens said, merely "notes" about "the incessant conjunctioning between things as they are and things imagined." Certain of his persistent symbols—especially, of course, the guitar, blue, sun and moon—reappear, and a number of the earlier themes and subjects are reworked, but none of the poems is developed with any complexity of detail. "Things as they are" is seen from various perspectives: in XXX it is a "banal suburb" and in XXXI the bickerings of employer and employes; in II and III it is a world that does not believe in the heroes the poet would create and that believes the truth is only in objective measurable fact; in XVI it is the earth as a hard world, as stone, not as a mother; and in XVII man is an "animal," not a "soul." Section XV, using Picasso's distortions of the man with the blue guitar, echoes those parts of *Owl's Clover* that present our world as one knowing no belief it can accept as true or meaningful. The poet, or any man of imagination, lives in his world but "patches it as he can."

In "The Statue at the World's End," Stevens had said that we "live incessantly in change." The time we call "serene" is a part of the movement. There are tragic lullabies, solemn and melancholy days, but the chaos slows into a "momentary calm" and there is "the sound of z in the grass all day." Should we trade this world, the one we know, for one we know not of?

> Shall you
> Then, fear a drastic community evolved
> From the whirling, slowly and by trial; or fear
> Men gathering for a mighty flight of men,
> An abysmal migration into a possible blue?

Some years later in *Esthétique du Mal* he made a similar, but more pointed, comment on the danger of attempting to force all the people to

> Live, work, suffer and die in that idea
> In a world of ideas.

The revolutionary who insists that his is *the* idea and argues his cause logically from it is a "logical lunatic."

>   The cause
> Creates a logic not to be distinguished
> From lunacy.

Later, in "Idiom of the Hero," from *Parts of a World*, he returns to this subject.

> I heard two workers say, "This chaos
> Will soon be ended."

The chaos, Stevens says, will never be ended. Nor will man, a part of the chaos, be "mended." This faith in the future, a substitute heaven, is a part of the leftist doctrine that caused him to write *Owl's Clover*. A half dozen poems, or parts of poems, in *Parts of a World* probe and question others among these doctrines.

In this volume, as in his work generally, he stresses the need for recognizing that we live in our sensibilities and the need for being wary of committing ourselves to a too strict rationalism. In "Forces, the Will and the Weather" he describes a day that lives through our senses, observing "There was not an idea This side of Moscow." And in "A Dish of Peaches in Russia" he attacks, by implication, the unnaturalness of attempting to give one's allegiance to an abstract system. In the color of the large, round peaches a Russian sees "the colors of my village." He discovers that

he is committed, by his affection, by his senses, to his village. He finds the part of himself that loves personally is at
war with the part that attempts to live impersonally. "Marx,"
Stevens wrote in *Ideas of Order*, "has ruined Nature, for
the moment." And in *Transport to Summer* he imagined
that

> Lenin on a bench beside a lake disturbed
> The swans. He was not a man for swans.

In "United Dames of America," from *Parts of a World*,
he attacks a related fallacy, the presenting of the concept of
"men in a mass." We can conceive only the individual face.
In "Extracts from Addresses to the Academy of Fine Ideas,"
III, from the same volume, he states, however, one of the
dangers of excessive individuality, for a society in which
"all men are priests." Excessive individualism precludes an
over-all design, such a design as that afforded by the me-
dieval Church. In the latter kind of world one would have
a sense of purpose, of "design." Is it, he seems to be asking,
that a society in which each man is his own priest prevents
the growth of a single thought on the basis of which the
individual could find meaning and could "savor" living?

On the other hand, "Life on a Battleship" makes it evident that, in seeing the virtues of a society with an over-all
design, Stevens is not unaware of the need for unity and
design by universal consent. The Captain, the figure in the
poem, considers the nature of the "ideal" state, the fool-
proof police state. First, he would build an enormous ship,
the largest "possible machine," to house all people. There
would be no other ships—and therefore no chance for other
states. As captain, he would be the divinity. This would be
the great simplification. The Captain, however, is aware of
a flaw. If it is the final simplification, the product of strict
rationality, why must it be "grandiose," why—with the bel-

lowing of commands and the firing of guns at the captain's command—must it be so similar to other societies, those held together by such symbols as the scepter or the crown? These are not rational—they are an opiate, or "make-believe." The Captain throws up the question. Second, he sees no reason to believe that the unity of the state or nation or race is more than a phase. In the great simplification the part (the Captain) would be equal to the whole, greater in fact by virtue of controlling the whole. The society in which the individual had a voice would be history.

The poet, at last, poses a problem for the Captain. "The whole cannot exist," he says, "without the parts," without the will of the parts. The "flaw" the Captain saw in employing symbols (which he calls "make-believe") is the very reason that the Captain could not carry out his plans. The Captain could exist as "divinity" for the parts only if the parts were to conceive him thus. Before that could be possible there would have to be a history, with martyrs, prophets, and stories, which would cause the parts to accept the Captain, a new "sceptre." Because unity is dependent upon our response to symbols "Our fate is our own."

Parts of a World, a book of sixty-five poems, has a thesis. A part of it is stated in "Asides on the Oboe":

> The prologues are over. It is a question, now,
> Of final belief.

In "Of Bright & Blue Birds and the Gala Sun" we are reminded that we possess not only "The will to be" but to be "total in belief." It is, as Stevens puts it in "Extracts from Addresses to the Academy of Fine Ideas," "a singular romance, This warmth in the blood-world for the pure idea." Singular or not, the desire is in us, and we search for the controlling idea, the interrelated body of beliefs in which we can feel at ease. The tragedy of our world is in our

> inability to find a sound
> That clings to the mind like that right sound . . . .

Put another way, the tragedy is our searching for an absolute belief in a world that does not believe in absolutes. We have killed the gods. All the old beliefs are questioned. Even, we read in "Mrs. Alfred Uruguay," many of the beliefs that some might feel would never be questioned.

> I fear that elegance
> Must struggle like the rest.

Does Stevens have an answer? Or, better, does he have an adequate answer? He does have an answer, but after a point it tends to be tenuous and vague. He acknowledges that beliefs are fictions, but holds that some fictions accord with our needs, like the fiction of heroism, nobility, love, or the brotherhood of man. We can believe in them even though we know that to some extent they are our own creations, that our desires, feelings and rituals help to create and sustain them. Having created them, we can live with them. Let us, then, says Stevens, acknowledge that in this world, which is alien to or at least unaware of man's aspirations, the

> final belief
> Must be in a fiction. It is time to choose . . . .

Does not this acknowledging our beliefs to be "fictions," however, leave us where we were, with the varied and conflicting beliefs which war on each other? It need not, Stevens seems to be saying, if we focus our attention on man, on

> The central man, the human globe, responsive
> As a mirror with a voice, the man of glass,
> Who in a million diamonds sums us up.

In other words, by attending to the nature of man and viewing him honestly we should be able to find a major belief, the belief acceptable and necessary to the "central man," "without external reference." This position is tenuous, obviously, because of the immediately faced difficulty of getting agreement on the nature of the "central man." At least, in working through *Parts of a World,* in which the word *centre* or *central* occurs about twenty times, we can discover what Stevens sees or would emphasize as needs of the natural man.

The speaker in "The Latest Freed Man" finds himself, once he has become aware that the strength of the sun is his strength and aware of the physical natural world, at "the centre of reality, seeing it." A persistent need, according to "Extracts from the Academy of Fine Ideas," is for

> Ecstatic identities
> Between one's self and the weather . . . .

Again, one wants to be able

> To face the weather and be unable to tell
> How much of it was light and how much thought . . . .

Accepting and being at ease in the physical world, then, would seem to be the "subtle centre" that Stevens sees as the need for the natural man.

The term—sometimes it is "essential" rather than "central"—is also used in other contexts, usually to mean a fundamental or primary consideration or, even, an abstraction that is a kind of synthesis. Thus, for example, in *Notes toward a Supreme Fiction,* he would have us conceive of the "idea of man" before he is transformed in our imaginations, or, in *A Primitive like an Orb,* the essential nature of poetry, not individual poems. This latter pursuit of the central takes us into broad abstractions, and, it would seem, farther and farther from union of thought and physical sensation.

This concern with finding a center suggests the kind of speculation to be found in the later poetry. The comments and speculations may be too tangential to allow us to call them philosophical, but they indicate the considerable extent to which Stevens' thought after *Harmonium* has been given over to the problem of belief and "order."

Despite the pointed wit, the ease of expression and the controlled rhythms, virtues which are constant in Stevens' work, *Parts of a World* is one of his least successful volumes. "Connoisseur of Chaos," "Life on a Battleship," and a few other poems in which there are a speculative manner and the working out of a thesis, are not very successful. Often one feels willing to exchange many of these poems, with their heavy import, for a poem similar in artistry to "Sea Surface Full of Clouds," in which the associations are fused into a magnificent symbol. The Stevens who wrote *Harmonium* was in possession of *a* world, the esthetic, but the Stevens of *Parts of a World* is in search of one.

Notes toward a Supreme Fiction is a further exploration of the way in which fiction, or the things of the imagination, and the real are dependent upon each other. There are, in each of three major sections, ten poems of twenty lines each. In the first section, "It Must Be Abstract," the poet attempts to suggest, in so far as we can conceive a world untouched by our imaginings, the nature of the world outside of man and prior to man. He would conceive the world without images, in "the idea of it," as an "abstraction blooded, as a man by thought." He would have us, then, conceive of "major man," not MacCullough, the individual man, but "the idea of man." If we can approach this idea of the world and man in this "candid" view of them we should thereafter be better able to see them in the plurality of the forms furnished us by the workings of the imagination.

In the second section, "It Must Change," he sees man as living in a "Theatre of Trope," transforming the things he sees, and giving a luminousness and emotional quality to the experiences he has. The transforming imaginings of the heart and mind, according to "Ozymandias," wrap the bride in a "fictive covering." In parodying Shelley's "Be thou me," Stevens humorously disposes of the fallacy of wanting to be identified with any one form of nature—only in change and in variation is there delight and enjoyment. The man who enjoys the changing colors of his world can bear his labors. The subtlety in pleasure is from variation.

In the final section, "It Must Give Pleasure," he sees two sources of pleasure, seeing things-as-they-are held to themselves, and seeing things-as-they-are changed by the imagination, the "fiction that results from feeling." For the former we may instance

> the way a leaf
> Above the table spins its constant spin,
> So that we look at it with pleasure, look
> At it spinning its eccentric measure.

For the latter, this:

> Bent over work, anxious, content, alone,
> You remain the more than natural figure. You
> Become the soft-footed phantom, the irrational
>
> Distortion, however fragrant, however dear.

Notes toward a Supreme Fiction, the exposition of three
major aspects of the ways in which we see the world, exhibits a rare and wonderful artistry. It is told in a language
that is discursive and subtle but which never for more than
a line or two fails to suggest and evoke, by image, connotation and inconspicuous rhythms, the realm of sensibility
in which our fictions are born.

The fifteen short sections of *Esthétique du Mal* (1944) were
written as answers to the question, How should the imagination respond to pain and evil? We must, first, the poet
answers, admit that pain is human—the earth might be con-
sumed in fire but only *we* would know the pain. The moon
and space are indifferent to our suffering, but because un-
involved with, or free from, us they cause us to accept and
live with things-as-they-are. Next, he considers the kind of
world we would experience if we did not have the capacity
for mistakes and for inviting misfortune—it would be a
pretty, sweet kind of world, like that of the sentimentalist.
In section V he discusses the consequences of a specific bit
of knowledge. Instinctively we love most fully our closest
kin, those with whom we have strong blood ties, but now
that we are "wholly human," now that we know about the
accidents of birth and physical appearances, the shadow of
our awareness falls between us and our family. Knowledge,
we may infer, is not unrelated to the forms of evil. Nor is
the ripeness possible in "the landscape of the sun" an unqualified good—what the sun brings to perfection it also
consumes. Again, the realist who has destroyed Satan and,
with him, many blue phenomena, wins a victory at great
expense: he wants from long habit to be able to affirm that
more than death, more than "cold vacancy," awaits him. If
the "death of Satan was a tragedy For the imagination" so

too has been our seeing the moon, once known as an agent furthering fertility and affecting man's mind, as a "lustred nothingness," or "comic ugliness." A part of the life of the sensibility is lost in payment for the new truth. In Section X the poet, employing his symbol of woman as the "grossly maternal," says that the maternal may afford great solace, even escape into a childlike innocence where we are impervious to "impersonal pain." Knowing the kind of escape offered is into a childlike unconsciousness, he is not free to accept it. Therefore he must live, as it were, next to a way of escape from pain which he never feels free to use. In the section beginning "Life is a bitter aspic," he comments on and illustrates the paradox that bitter experience caught in the "gaiety of language" satisfies a part of our hunger for enjoyment. The poem ends on this: there is great pain in our physical existence, but consider the delight in the "many selves" and "sensuous worlds" that our experience of evil and good makes possible.

Esthétique du Mal, despite its fine passages, its frequently wonderful facility in bringing seemingly tangential insights into focus about a general point, is not one of Stevens' most successful long poems. Its language lacks the masculine vigor of "The Comedian as the Letter C," the subtle richness of *Notes toward a Supreme Fiction* or the more obvious richness of "Credences of Summer." This subject, it would seem, does not engage his imagination so powerfully as his other subjects. Among the general criticisms one might make of the poem are these: Evil too often is treated thematically, not as actual painful experience; and only limited aspects of the subject are examined. The sections in their arrangement too often are discrete. Most readers are likely to see Section XII as the kind of intellectual legerdemain into which Stevens' genius for language seldom betrays him.

The number of those poems that touch on political ques-

tions and the social order should not be taken to indicate
that Stevens believes, as do some of his contemporaries,
that politics must play a necessary part in the role of the
poet. "I might be expected," he writes in "The Noble
Rider and the Sound of Words," "to speak of the social,
that is to say sociological or political obligation of the poet.
He has none." He does admit that a social or political matter *may* move a poet. Poetry is a matter of the imagination,
what appeals to it and stirs it. It is not the servant of politics. "Stalin might grind his teeth the whole of a Russian
winter and yet all the poets in the Soviets might remain
silent the following spring. He might excite their imaginations by something he said or did. He would not command
them." In the same essay he says that the social and political obligation many attempt to force on the poet is a contemporary phenomenon. Once, in answering a series of
questions for *Twentieth Century Verse*, October, 1938, he
said the younger American poets lacked a leader, that "the
fury of poetry always comes from the presence of a mad-
man or two," but "at the moment all the madmen are poli-
ticians."

In fact, for Stevens the preoccupation with politics forced
upon us by the developments of our time is a part of the
"pressure of reality" against which the poet's imagination
must press back. The poet's function is not to lead people
along the way of political righteousness. The poet's function
is to see and speak imaginatively: "he fulfills himself only
as he sees his imagination become the light in the minds of
others."

VI

The Unthinking Source

STEVENS IS an intellectual poet. A part of his strength lies in his capacity for fine distinctions, for subtlety. "It is of our nature," he says, "that we proceed from the chromatic to the clear, from the unknown to the known." He has praised those who are "shapers," who help to bring order out of disorder. A "constant shaping . . . is characteristic of the poet." And he has praised those who through intelligence and discipline achieve precise statements. It is also true, however, that he has written such lines as these, from *Owl's Clover:*

> We have grown weary of the man that thinks.
> He thinks and it is not true.

Such a seeming paradox, a poet who is at once an intellectual and a hater of ideas, a misologist, implies a strange contradiction in the poet himself, or else the paradox has been created through the misunderstanding of some of his critics.

Stevens has the awareness, as also had Schopenhauer and Nietzsche, that rationality can no longer be safely considered the sole key to the understanding and explanation of the human role. Questions of the nature and destiny of man not only in terms of the eternal but in terms of the temporal, and involving the social, political, moral, psychological, and esthetic, have been seen in startlingly different perspectives. The old dichotomy on the basis of which rationality was seen to be in opposition to irrationality now seems an oversimplification. This is not the occasion to examine this tradition,[1] but it is quite apparent that Stevens' "subman," for example, is related to Darwin's "will to survive," Bergson's "élan vital," and Freud's "id," all of which in turn were products of a Zeitgeist in which "educated and sensitive people throughout Europe [had] become aware of the depredations the reason might make upon the affective life." Stevens' concern with our participating in nature has none of the deep pessimism to be found in Schopenhauer's "will to live," in our being caught up by a shapeless force that betrays us into rationalizations that merely support the innumerable desires growing out of our will to survive. Nor does this concern lead him into Nietzsche's self-conscious and somewhat frenzied desire for a union with nature through the good offices of Dionysus. Yet there are certain similarities to be observed. Stevens' "Imagination is the will of things," perhaps the key to all his poetry, indicates his desire and concern to be involved in nature, or actively a part of it. Stevens' phrase "Earth, the drunken mother" obviously is closely akin to Nietzsche's "drunken reality." In "Crude Foyer," from *Transport to Summer,* he says the "landscape" thought opens to us always "turns out to be here." This could have been placed as an epigraph at the head of a section of *The Birth of Tragedy* in which Nietzsche speaks of the pursuits of the theoretician, whose

[1] See, e.g., Lionel Trilling, "Freud and Literature," *The Kenyon Review,* Spring, 1941. Many of the figures that would belong in such an examination are to be found in this article.

illusion consists in the imperturbable belief that, with the
clue of logic, thinking can reach to the nethermost depths
of being, and that thinking cannot only perceive being but
even modify it. This sublime metaphysical illusion is added
as an instinct to science and again must change into *art;
which is really the end to be attained by this mechanism.*

Thought, like physical existence, is a part of a "drifting
waste." In "Fabliau of Florida" we are envisioned as living
in a world of foam and cloud, and "Sea Surface Full of
Clouds" extends the symbol. The changes in the surface of
the sea and in the poet's mind observing them are dependent upon the "sovereign clouds." Our thoughts come to
focus out of the mists just as the day or night or a change
in the weather is seen to come to focus in "Variations on a
Summer Day," from *Parts of a World,* through the shifting
of the clouds:

> The cloudy world, by aid of land and sea,
> Night and day, wind and quiet, produces
> More nights, more days, more clouds, more worlds.

The "floribund ascetic," in "Landscape with Boat," is advised that in his search for truth he should pause to consider that he himself may be a part of the truth and the
clouds a part of the truth.

In "The Lack of Repose," from *Transport to Summer,* a
young man reads a book referred to as "a cloud in which a
voice mumbles," and its author is called "a ghost that in-
habits a cloud." The frothy clouds are a part of the real
world, giving delight to the "blue woman, linked and lac-
quered, at her window," or to Jocundus, the man who
enjoys his speculations about the world yet never forgets
that he lives primarily in his sensibilities because he lives in
a physical world.

Quite frequently Stevens reminds us that in aspiring to know the Truth as a single entity or as a principle informing all knowledge or awarenesses we may overlook the obvious, that the physical world is a part of the truth. Thus from "On the Road Home," from *Parts of a World:*

> It was when I said,
> "There is no such thing as the truth,"
> That the grapes seemed fatter.
> The fox ran out of his hole.

Several additional poems in the same volume stress the sense of well being that goes at times with merely existing in the warmth of the sun ("The Latest Freed Man"), in the evening light ("A Rabbit as King of the Ghosts"), or on a summer day ("Forces, the Will and the Weather").

In "Pieces," from *Transport to Summer,* he says, "There are things in a man besides his reason." There seems to be, for example, "a sense in sounds beyond their meaning." There are significances in various aspects of being which we feel but cannot articulate. It may be, he continues in the first section of *Notes toward a Supreme Fiction,* VII, that the "truth depends on a walk around a lake," allowing a definition to grow by itself within the mind, and the body to enjoy moments that have fortuitously come to "a kind of Swiss perfection." The poems that compose "Credences of Summer" further develop this search for a center, an "axis of everything," in the physical world. In summer, when nature comes to its greenest and our days in their colors and ripeness are at their best, there is such a center. "The utmost must be good and is." For Stevens, there is no Providence responsible for these delights.

The only god that Stevens names is Ananke (Necessitas), the force to which all else must yield. In "The

Greenest Continent," from *Owl's Clover*, Ananke is presented as the "final god," as

> that obdurate ruler who ordains
> For races, not for men, powerful beyond
> A grace to nature, a changeless element.

It is appropriate, Stevens says in "Less and Less Human, O Savage Spirit," from *Transport to Summer*, that if "There must be a god in the house" he be alien to us. The god of "Credences of Summer" is an "inhuman author" who cannot hear his characters speak. It is right that this be so, Stevens says in *Esthétique du Mal*, so we may give our attention to the earth:

> It seems as if the honey of common summer
> Might be enough.

The universe, too, whether terrifying or beautiful, is inhuman. One may come to terms with some of the terror. One may, for example, by studying the trees covered with ice and listening to the wind develop a "mind of winter." In "The Comedian as the Letter C," he speaks of an "inscrutable universe."

Sometimes, too, as in *Esthétique du Mal*, he pauses to consider the existence of evil, suffering and death. But usually, for Stevens, it is a good as well as mysterious universe. "Sweet berries ripen in the wilderness." The sense of the mystery of existence remains almost constant. Even loneliness or fear is arrested and held in the middle distance for our esthetic delight, as in the early "Thirteen Ways of Looking at a Blackbird."

> Among twenty snowy mountains
> The only moving thing
> Was the eye of the blackbird.

There is a similar, equal magic in the later "No Possum, No Sop, No Taters," from *Transport to Summer*.

We ourselves are a mysterious part of nature. Thanks to our mysterious sensibilities, we may view and delight in our relationship to the rest of nature, either lyrically or ironically. Man is flesh, a "mincing gobbet."

Two figures in the mythology of Stevens' poetry which seem to be closely associated and his own personal creations are Chocorua and Hoon. Chocoru, a mountain in Vermont, has a place in New England legends. The story is that a white hunter pursued an Indian chief, who leapt from a precipice and was killed. But this story, which may have suggested the symbol to Stevens, is not necessary to an understanding of the meaning of Chocorua in his poems. In them, it has become the mountain of the self, huge and shadowy because of the power of the imagination to magnify and to soar in an immense heaven of its own creation, but it also is of this earth, the "flesh, the bone, the dirt, the stone." Hoon functions somewhat similarly. It suggests solitariness, detachment, indifference to human imaginings. Ironically, it is also a part of the self.

The most persistent symbol of the unthinking sources of life in Stevens' poetry is the sun. In *Harmonium* the sun is a constant symbol. He calls it "That strange flower, the sun." The thesis of "Sunday Morning" is, in effect, that if we were to come to terms with the universe and to create a religion that had its paradise on earth we would "chant in orgy on a summer morn," make our devotions to the sun, as though it were a "savage source." And "From the Misery of Don Joost" states that when the body finishes its "combat with the sun" it "knows nothing more." In "Anatomy of Monotony" man is seen as "naked in the sun."

We are, in a sense, the sun. If in "Life Is Motion," also from *Harmonium*, Bonnie and Josie dance around a stump it is as celebrants of the life source, and as participants in "the marriage of flesh and air." In a number of poems marriage itself is celebrated in similar terms, never as an institution nor in sociological, economic or moral terms.

Most often, it is treated, by implication, as a part of another persistent symbol, woman:

> Night, the female,
> Obscure,
> Fragrant and supple . . . .

(In "The Comedian as the Letter C" woman, in this sense, is "my blonde.") The male lover in "Last Look at Lilacs" is advised in ironic terms not to pause in the "hymeneal air" for intellectual commentaries but to be "arrogantly male." In the third section of *Notes toward a Supreme Fiction*, IV, there is the marriage of a great captain and Bawda. They marry well because both love the place, Catawba, in which they live. Of Bawda it is said she "loved the captain as she loved the sun." And in the second section of the same poem, VIII, one Nanzia Nunzio, "the spouse," is shown confronting Ozymandias. She would learn how to perfect herself as the "contemplated spouse." The point here is that as such she is a part of the nature of things; in Stevens' dramatis personae, an aspect of woman as fecundity, one of the dark sources of life. Again, in *Esthétique du Mal*, X, he seeks the "grossly maternal," not the "*mauve* Maman," because she is "reality." An earlier poem, "The Woman That Had More Babies Than That," from *Parts of a World*, states that all of us, even the "old men" and the "philosophers," listening to the mysterious sound of the sea are haunted by the maternal voice and the soothing "explanation" at night. A permanent human desire is "for the fiery lullaby."

A somewhat similar figure is the "subman," opposed to

the rationalist or the man who merely thinks. In "Sombre Figuration," from *Owl's Clover*, he is characterized most explicitly:

> There is a man whom rhapsodies of change,
> Of which he is the cause, have never changed
> And never will, a subman under all
> The rest, to whom in the end the rest return,
> The man below the man below the man,
> Steeped in night's opium, evading day.

He does not live according to rules of logic. He is, as it were, the natural man, primitive and almost vegetative, but, by transforming what he sees into something else, as the bell into a church or a cry into a person, he keeps us living in a fluid, changing world. Without him there would be a static, changeless order.

One might, with some justification, feel that the world of Stevens' dramatis personae tends to exhibit a too peaceful version of human experience, to be somewhat passive. Among them, however, is the soldier, the figure who reminds us that we live in a world of movement that is unreasoning and that we, a part of it, are often irrational. In *Harmonium* the soldier is an infrequent figure, but he is seen as he will be in the later volumes. After he falls, in "The Death of the Soldier," the winds stop but

> The clouds go, nevertheless,
> In their direction . . . .

There is a fatalism about the death of soldiers in "Dry Loaf," from *Parts of a World*. Spring by spring, the birds come like waves flowing in the sky. They come like the soldiers, marching, marching, marching.

It was soldiers went marching over the rocks
And still the birds came, came in watery flocks,
Because it was spring and the birds had to come.
No doubt that soldiers had to be marching
And that drums had to be rolling, rolling, rolling.

But the wound of the soldier in *Esthétique du Mal*, VII, is found to be "good because life was." The soldier of time, all soldiers who live vigorously and well, sleeps as though in a "summer sleep." Similarly the soldiers of "Giganto-machia" and "Dutch Graves in Bucks County," both from *Transport to Summer*, go to their deaths well because they lived lives larger than themselves as individuals. The sol-dier, like woman and the subman, lives and moves instinc-tively, like the clouds or the birds. He unquestioningly expresses, as it were, the will of nature.

This emphasis in Stevens' poetry upon the unthinking source as an elemental and to a great extent a controlling factor in our existence makes readily understandable the attention he gives to the physical, places, animals, birds, in-sects, vegetation and growth. In at least two poems he calls existence in an immaterial heaven the "greatest poverty."

Frequently his poems are heavy with a sense of physical being. Thus in "Frogs Eat Butterflies. Snakes Eat Frogs. Hogs Eat Snakes. Men Eat Hogs," from *Harmonium*:

        the rivers went nosing like swine,
    Tugging at banks, until they seemed
    Bland belly-sounds in somnolent troughs. . . .

Or "Description of a Platonic Person," from *Transport to Summer*:

    Then came Brazil to nourish the emaciated
    Romantic with dreams of her avoirdupois, green glade
    Of serpents like Z rivers simmering.

John Finch, in "North and South in Stevens' America," [2] has shown that in *Harmonium* there is a "precision to Stevens' geography," not merely an "array of pleasantly clattering syllables." Florida, "venereal soil," is tropical warmth, deep colors, vegetative and sensuous existence. It is a land of dark blue night skies, the droning surf, brightly hued birds, yellow sun, and quick growth. Several poems in *Harmonium*—"Fabliau of Florida," "O Florida, Venereal Soil," "Stars at Tallapoosa," "Two Figures in Dense Violet Night," "Indian River," and "Nomad Exquisite"—are explicitly concerned with Florida as a land of the imagination. The "green vine angering for life," the "lightning colors" and the "blessed mornings" cause the beholder to bring forth "hymn" after "hymn." Places in Central and South America, as well as Cuba and the Carolinas, named and unnamed, function similarly. The treatment of the imagination in relation to the sea in "Sea Surface Full of Clouds" is set in "November off Tehuantepec." Mexico and Yucatan are the tropical setting opposed to the cold, icy north of New England in "The Comedian as the Letter C." Stevens himself, beginning with "Farewell to Florida," from *Ideas of Order*, accepts the north as home for him.

In Part IV of "The Comedian as the Letter C," Stevens noted: "his soil is man's intelligence" and "The natives of the rain are rainy men." Scattered through his books are occasional poems recognizing the determining forces of environment. The paradoxical "Theory" catches an aspect of the matter:

I am what is around me.

Women understand this.
One is not a duchess
A hundred yards from a carriage.

[2] *Harvard Advocate*, Dec., 1940, pp. 23–26.

In "The Latest Freed Man," from *Parts of a World*, one "bathes in the mist like a man without a doctrine." The man's strength is from the sun: through this he came to be free, and through it he finds himself at "the centre of reality."

The blackmen of "The Greenest Continent," from *Owl's Clover*, illustrate most fully Stevens' thesis that the religion and art of men is from their soil. The religion of the north, where "Jerusalem is Glasgow-frost or Paris rain," is not that of Africa. Nor can the art of the north be the art of Africa. The marble

> horses are part of a northern sky
> Too starkly pallid for the jaguar's light,
> In which he and the lion and the serpent hide
> Even in sleep, deep in the grass of sleep,
> Deep grass that totters under the weight of light.

Religion and art develop forms peculiar to the soil in which they germinate and grow. This is not a matter of choice or design; it is as though Ananke

> caused the statue to be made
> And he will fix the place where it will stand.

Earlier, in "Anecdote of Men by the Thousand," from *Harmonium*, he had investigated the same theme. The soul

> is composed
> Of the external world.

Manners and style take at least a part of their character from the place from which they arise.

The references to physical being, as one might expect, are fairly constant in the various volumes. Animals: frogs, snakes, pigs, firecats, jaguars, lions, elephants, and horses. Birds: red birds, blackbirds, tanagers, parrots, peacocks, swans, pigeons, flamingos, pheasants, doves, cocks, grackles, and buzzards. Insects: butterflies, moths, crickets, spiders, and ants. Again, there is vegetation of all kinds. Trees: pine, palm, palmetto, hemlock, juniper, orange, spruce, dogwood, and magnolia. Fruits and plants: pineapple, plum, banana, pear, peach, berries, mango, apricot, watermelon, bougainvillea, gourds, cabbage, and radish. Flowers: lilac, iris, geranium, canna, hydrangea, melon-flower, acacia, hepatica, forsythia, larkspur, rose, and jasmine. A poet's imagery is held a clue to the nature of his interest and vision. The range and frequency of the images of physical life and growth in Stevens is evidence, more than enough, of his preoccupation with the physical world.

The early "Stars at Tallapoosa" suggests, despite its partial obscurity, the reason for this preoccupation. Rationality, like the straight lines between the stars, is merely a part of human experience. Centering upon rationality alone leads to oversimplification, to ignoring the dark night that envelops the lines between the stars. The body "is an eye that studies its black lid." The life of the sensibilities is not in the straight lines alone, in rationality. To insist that it is will prevent "recoveries of young nakedness" and the "vehemence the midnights hold."

VII

Imagination as the Will of Things

COLERIDGE, FRUSTRATED in his love for Sarah Hutchinson, wrote "Dejection: An Ode" (1802) to express his sadness over the consequent loss of his "sole resource," "his only plan"—"My shaping spirit of Imagination." Without it he is heavy spirited, joyless; for Imagination

> is the spirit and the power,
> Which, wedding Nature to us, gives in dower
> A new Earth and new Heaven,
> Undreamt of by the sensual and the proud:
> Joy is the sweet voice, Joy the luminous cloud:
> We in ourselves rejoice!
> And thence flows all that charms or ear or sight,
> All melodies the echoes of that voice,
> All colours a suffusion from that light.

For Coleridge the imagination is under the aegis of, or symbolized by, the moon.[1] He has been called "moonstruck," and his philosophy, by his detractor Carlyle, "bottled moonshine." A few years ago, Robert Penn Warren

---

[1] "Sonnet to the Autumnal Moon" (1788), "Christabel" (1797–1816), "Kubla Khan" (1798–1811), "The Nightingale" (1798), "Song of the Pixies" (1796), etc.

worked out the significance of the moon symbolism as a part of his detailed analysis of *The Rime of the Ancient Mariner*.[2] He points out that in *Biographia Literaria*, XIV, Coleridge equates moonlight with the "modifying-colours of the imagination" and that in other places the moon is associated with man's imaginative relationship with Nature. Mr. Warren observes these instances in preparation for examining the symbolism of the moon as a part of the symbolic structure and as part of the meaning of *The Rime of the Ancient Mariner*. Imagination in the context of the poem is seen in its "value-creating capacity," which Coleridge would later call the "secondary imagination." The sun is equated with events that represent understanding, rationality, practicality, and so forth.[3] The moon is equated with events that represent the creative imagination. It develops, in Mr. Warren's reading, that the crime against the Albatross is not a crime against the "sacramental universe" alone, but a crime against the creative imagination. To attempt to live solely by the understanding or by the reason is to attempt to live abstractly, outside of nature.[4] For Coleridge to commit himself to the imagination in a world that was coming more and more to emphasize scientific-mindedness and practicality and to dismiss both communings with nature and esthetic concerns was to invite ridicule. Coleridge has been among the few voices in the past several centuries to win much of a hearing for the imagination. Certainly the realm of imagination is not easily delimited or defined, but Coleridge was able, whatever the limitations of his statements, through his emphasis on the "esemplastic sense," his seeing imagination as the agent of the sensibility, his separating fancy from imagination, and so

[2] New York, Reynal and Hitchcock, 1946. See especially pp. 86–100.
[3] See *Biographia Literaria*, I.
[4] There was of course behind Coleridge a history of this kind of rationalism. It is in Bacon, Hobbes, Locke, Descartes, and many others. See, e.g., Basil Willey, *The Seventeenth Century Background*.

forth, to suggest that we possess faculties that are creative and not to be reined in tightly by the Hobbesian "judgment" and "reason."

The point, of course, in introducing this brief sketch of Coleridge's concern with imagination is to connect it with Stevens' emphasis on the role of imagination. Coleridge wrote in opposition to a rationalist tradition, and so does Stevens. This is not to say that their theories of the imagination are identical. Coleridge at certain points relates the imagination to the supernatural; Stevens does not. Coleridge believes the power of imagination is denied to the "sensual and the proud"; there is no reason to think that Stevens does.

There are, on the other hand, obvious similarities between their positions. Both oppose the imaginative to the rationalist mind. Both see imagination as the way of establishing communion with nature and enjoying it in the transformed shapes and colors the imagination makes possible. And both employ light, particularly the moon and stars, as a symbol of the imaginative faculties.

In his earliest poems Stevens discusses an opposition as well as the relationship between objective reality and the imagination. "Colloquy with a Polish Aunt," from *Harmonium*, states what in effect is Stevens' theme epitomized: "Imagination is the will of things." "Another Weeping Woman" makes the same point in a more paradoxical fashion. Through "The Idea of Order at Key West" we are shown that the world exists for us only as it exists in our minds. This theme had been treated earlier, as in "Sea Surface Full of Clouds." The stillness or the varied movements of the sea in the morning, at noon, or evening, and the lights playing through the water suggest subtly shifting motives and moods—all of course attributed to it by the imagination of the poet. It is a multihued and teasingly ambiguous world for those with perception and imagination. The ennui and tedium of those, as in "Disillusionment of Ten O'Clock," whose houses are haunted by white nightgowns is of their own making. The goddess reigning over *Harmonium* is "One of Fictive Music."

This faith in the imagination of the individual should not tempt us to look to the poet as one who can raise us above the problems of reality, to some realm of imagination in which there are no burdensome problems. Stevens writes in the first section of "The Man With the Blue Guitar" that the poet plays

> A tune beyond us, yet ourselves
>
> A tune upon the blue guitar
> Of things exactly as they are.

Stevens is aware, much more keenly than most of his contemporaries, that *reality* in our time is used honorifically, associated with such ideals as practicality, objectivity and rationality; he is aware, that is, of the old dichotomy between objectivity and subjectivity, between reality and appearance. Stevens knows, as anyone should who stops to consider the matter, that in our minds the two are never separate. We feel about an object according to our beliefs, our likes and dislikes. Whether the image of it in our mind is to be labeled *true* or *illusory* will depend to a considerable extent on the beliefs, likes and dislikes in the mind of the one doing the labeling. Is there really a separation between imagination and things-as-they-are? To a limited extent, to the extent that we can transform both the world and our experiences, he says in effect in Section XXII, we may say that imagination "gives" as well as receives from reality or things-as-they-are. In Section V his ambitions for the poet are greater. Like Matthew Arnold he would have the poet be a great myth-maker.

Poetry

Exceeding music must take the place
Of empty heaven and its hymns.

Ourselves in poetry must take their place.

Years earlier, in "A High-Toned Old Christian Woman"
from *Harmonium*, he had called poetry "the supreme fiction," by which he meant that a belief becomes intelligible
and moving when it informs images, when it creates a
mythology. Thus belief of a certain kind, he says, gives
rise to churches, palm trees become symbols, a heaven is
created and peopled. The imagination creates a pantheon.
It can function in the service of religion or poetry. Simply
because the imagination serves the "moral law" should not
lead us to suppose, he continues, that it is solely in the
service of morality or religion. It can create a myth in the
service of an amoral or irreligious principle. For a "nave" it
can substitute a "peristyle" and for "heaven" a "masque."
These observations, he concludes,

will make widows wince. But fictive things
Wink as they will. Wink most when widows wince.

But the poet, however desirous he may be to find a belief
in which he might be at ease, cannot by taking thought
and then putting his imagination at the service of a belief
proceed to assist in the creation of a myth. There are forces
in a people larger and greater than the poet and in which
he participates. Stevens symbolizes a part of these forces
under the figure he calls the "subman."

Stevens' "subman," adumbrated in "This Brave Man" in
Ideas of Order but not developed until *Owl's Clover*, is not
only collective but antecedent to the "poet" or the "musician." He is a race, or a people who have lived with an in-

terrelated body of beliefs, with a myth. In their manners, their songs, their aspirations, or their style, are to be found the continuous *meanings* with which they live.

> The future for them is always the deepest dome,
> The darkest blue of the dome and the wings around
> The giant Phosphor of their earliest prayers.

Stevens emphasizes the subman, which he opposes to the abstract man, the "Johnsonian composition," because it is necessary to understand him. To emphasize the abstract man of the rationalists causes us to ignore or neglect this "man below" who lives

> in less
> Than body and in less than mind, ogre,
> Inhabitant, in less than shape, of shapes
> That are dissembled in vague memory
> Yet still retain resemblances, remain
> Remembrances, a place of a field of lights,
> As a church is a bell and people are an eye,
> A cry, the pallor of a dress, a touch.
> He turns us into scholars, . . .

He also turns us into poets. The poet or the musician is any man of imagination. Sometimes Stevens calls him the "orator." The poet is aware that he is a part of the subman, and that he lives in the "cat-eyed atmosphere" and in fluid movement. But the poet also knows, as Stevens states in "Holiday in Reality," from *Transport to Summer,* that to be individually alive or "real," each has "To find for himself his earth, his sky, his sea."

Coleridge, of course, distinguished between the primary and secondary imagination. Only the secondary was associated or, as he would say, coexisted with "the conscious

will." Thus the imagination of Stevens' "subman," although
not seen as "repetition in the finite mind of the eternal act
of creation in the Infinite I Am," is quite similar to Coleridge's primary imagination. It might be noted also that
imagination in its value-creating capacity, held by Coleridge to be a function of the secondary imagination, is an
essential concern with Stevens.

The subman, the man who imagines, creates the masks
that symbolize belief, the forms which come to seem permanent, solid and in the nature of things. The "sterile rationalist" and the stolidly unimaginative forget that the
forms, the styles, are the results of earlier imaginings.

> The solid was an age, a period
> With appropriate, largely English, furniture,
> Barbers with charts of the only possible modes,
> Cities that would not wash away in the mist . . . .

The complex forms of a culture come up out of the mist of
the mind. Given objective form, they become tangible
reality. In our Alexandrian age, however, we recognize that
the masks are our own imaginings.

> We perceive each mask
> To be the musician's own and, thence, become
> An audience to mimics . . . .

A sense of solidity, of order, is necessary. But order is not
possible, nor are the forms that evolve from it and in turn
stabilize it, if there is no large, controlling and informing
belief. An age of belief has gone. "The cycle of the solid
having turned," we are left with a sense of the possible
rightness of many varied beliefs, or with the sense that beliefs are fictions.

The world is seen as a changing theater, as in "Of Modern Poetry" from *Parts of a World:*

> Then the theatre was changed
> To something else. Its past was a souvenir.

The theater in this sense—as a period, its institutions, its art, and its way of life—is found in a number of poems. Two of them in *Transport to Summer,* "Repetitions of a Young Captain" and "Chaos in Motion and Not in Motion," use this figure. The former poem emphasizes that our world, the theater of the twentieth century, is in ruins, that we must rediscover what is of central importance in reality before a new theater can be erected.

Style is not something superficial, a manner superimposed on a basically unchanged reality. It expresses the beliefs and attitudes, created or formed though these are in various ways, of a man, or of a people and their time. Style, which is merely affected by the workings of rationality, arises in that part of our being that we label sensibility, and expresses not only our perceptions but our desires, aspirations, loves, hates and fears. The "subman" as well as the "musician" or the "poet," according to Stevens, gives form to this style.

From the first, Stevens has acknowledged his concern with style as well as his recognition that such a concern is commonly ignored or frowned upon. "The Weeping Burgher" from *Harmonium* is troubled about this acknowledgment and this recognition.

> It is with a strange malice
> That I distort the world . . . .

The verities are "sorry verities." We are reconciled to them by "excess," by style. He admits that he is "tortured for old speech," for the lost worlds of elegance—for a world that

knew "a black barouche." This, a theme to which Stevens
frequently returns, is found in "Lions in Sweden" from
Ideas of Order and "The Prejudice Against the Past" from
Transport to Summer.

There are frequent references to objects that have their
place in the lives of connoisseurs—barbaric glass, porcelain
or majolica; to the names and works of sculptors and
painters—Verrocchio, Franz Hals, Cézanne, Braque, Picasso,
Corot, Boucher or Marchand; and to musicians—Mozart
and Bach, or Shostakovitch. Even the world before man, or
imagined without man, is seen, in part, to have

> weather by Franz Hals,
> Brushed up by brushy winds in brushy clouds,
> Wetted by blue, colder for white.

In writing about the relation of imagination to nobility or
the attitudes of a society, as in *Owl's Clover* or "The Noble
Rider," Stevens' symbol or illustration is likely to be an art
object, in these instances, statues. That Stevens was never
taken in by the twentieth-century cult of "reality" is demonstrated readily by his acceptance of the reality of the imagination, its workings and its products. The imagination has,
of course, created the magnificence of Renaissance architecture or Augustan urbanity. John Malcolm Brinnin [5] has
pointed to the eighteenth-century décor in *Harmonium* and
some of the later volumes: citherns, claviers, lutes, wigs, para-
sols, salvers, tiaras, flambeaux, terraces, duchesses, masques,
peristyles, barouches, ribands. Taken collectively these *"objets d'art* of another century eminently represent the imagination in tangible artifact." "Floral Decorations for Bananas,"
from *Harmonium,* and "The Prejudice Against the Past"
from *Transport to Summer* may be the most explicit state-

5 "Plato, Phoebus and the Man from Hartford," *Voices,* No. 121
(Spring, 1945), 30–37.

ment of the need, as Stevens has felt it, for creating an elegant, urbane world.

Stevens is concerned with style both as a poet and as a student of the imagination. His reputation for many years was as a stylist alone, as though he were concerned with words or with style *per se*. Edmund Wilson, for example, once called him "a charming decorative artist." He has been accused of mere verbal legerdemain, as though a style worthy of acclaim could be created that expressed an insubstantial or, almost, a nonexistent subject matter. During that early period of his career, of course, writers were striving to be simple and direct: the naïve ideal was to get beneath style to the essential subject. Content was real. Style, thought of as rhetoric, was artificial. A style that hinted at the grand manner, even though checked by self-mockery, was suspect. With these attitudes toward style Stevens has been strongly in disagreement.

In "Description Without Place," from *Transport to Summer*, Stevens writes of the style of an era. An age, emphasizing certain beliefs, ignoring others, has a collective manner, a style. "An age is green or red." New "seemings," similar to those of Calvin or Anne of England, are always possible. A mind like Lenin's seeing the world contemporaneous with him as decadent could see the future as apocalyptic. Our description of a world, which is not an actual transcript of it, is intense because involved in it are our expectations and desires. In style, in other words, there is an expression of character. The "mountainous character" of the hidalgo is in his speech and in the design of his hat. The character of a whole nation may be caught in a phrase. The way in which we speak of the past or of the future is not to be taken lightly. In our description of the past we are forming our own character, and what we say of the future will have its consequences. Our "seemings" will influence later "seemings"—

Like rubies reddened by rubies reddening.

Color too can be a product of the imagination and a part
of style. In "The Man With the Blue Guitar," X, he sees

> color like a thought that grows
> Out of a mood . . . .

Stevens has from the beginning used color both descrip-
tively and in support of his theme or subject. Thus in
"Sunday Morning":

> Complacencies of the peignoir, and late
> Coffee and oranges in a sunny chair,
> And the green freedom of a cockatoo
> Upon a rug mingle to dissipate
> The holy hush of ancient sacrifice.
> She dreams a little, and she feels the dark
> Encroachment of that old catastrophe,
> As a calm darkens among water-lights.
> The pungent oranges and bright, green wings
> Seem things in some procession of the dead,
> Winding across wide water, without sound.

In "Disillusionment of Ten O'Clock" brightly colored
nightgowns symbolize a highly imaginative style and way
of life, and the active, adventurous life of the sailor is
"red weather." To know the world is to know it in its color.
The Yucatan Stevens shows us in "The Comedian as the
Letter C" has "raspberry tanagers," "green joys," "orange
air"—it is a world of "savage color." "Landscape With Boat,"
from Parts of a World, is a protest against the "floribund
ascetic" who thinks of truth as being outside himself and
as "colorless." If he could accept himself as a part of the
truth he could be more at ease in his world; he might sit

on a balcony at the shore of the Mediterranean, watching the emerald sea, the green palm leaves, and studying a "yellow wine." Stevens' poems are filled with images of color: "bright chromes," "pool of pink," "white pigeon," "blue pigeon," "golden gourds," "bronze rain," "beachy floors," "icy haze," "purple maws," "final slate," "emerald star," "yellow green," "comic colors," "a brune figure," "milky blue," "green roses," and innumerable others. Many of them recur and are played with not only to give a sense of the physical world but to give the language of the poetry an ambiguity that holds together and mutually comple-ments Stevens' most persistent themes.

Green, for example, is used to suggest *livingness* and our involvement in the physical world. When in "Sombre Figu-ration" Stevens wishes to suggest these things he writes:

> Green is the path we take
> Between chimeras and garlanded the way,
> The down-descent into November's void.

The mind of the scholar in "Chocorua to Its Neighbor" is a "Green mind" bulging "with complicated hues." In "Rep-etitions of a Young Captain," the need for rediscovering reality is stated:

> Green is the orator
> Of our passionate height. He wears a tufted green,
> And tosses green for those for whom green speaks . . . .

There are many similar instances, especially in *Transport to Summer*.

There are also a number of color usages in Stevens which suggest his awareness of color as the Impressionists were aware of it—that color is not in the object itself (the black bark of a tree) but varies not only with the light but with the position of the beholder (the tree may appear purple, or gray, or bronze). One of these instances is found early in "Of the Surface of Things," from *Harmonium*. The poet from his balcony surveys "the yellow air." And in the final stanza we read, "The gold tree is blue." This may be read in two ways; first, that the gold tree as seen from the balcony appears blue, or, second, the gold tree, a symbol of the beautiful in nature, is "blue" in the sense that Stevens himself uses the term, either as a symbol of the imagination or something connected with it.

Blue, with many connotations, ranges from the imaginative (as opposed to the realistic) to our most intense desires. It may be true, as Hi Simons[6] has attempted to demonstrate, that Stevens is indebted to Mallarmé, who frequently employed *azur* as a symbol of the ideal, the beautiful or the poetical. Simons has also shown that after 1919 Stevens uses blue consistently as a symbol. At first he uses it, as in "Banal Sojourn," "Fabliau of Florida," and "Homunculus et la belle étoile," in conjunction with "heaven" or "night" or "sky," but in "Of the Surface of Things" and "Colloquy with a Polish Aunt" he employed it with only attenuated suggestions of darkness. Thereafter one will find that it connotes poetry, the romantic, or the life of sensibilities, but most often imagination. In *Ideas of Order* it appears in such phrases as these: "mistiest blue of the lake," "bluest reason," "hole of blue," "broadest blue," and the future "blued." It is of course a part of the central symbol in "The Man With the Blue Guitar." In addition to the many incidental uses of it throughout, there is one section, XIII, in which it is the central symbol:

> The pale intrusions into blue
> Are corrupting pallors . . . ay di mi,

[6] "Wallace Stevens and Mallarmé," *Modern Philology*, XLIII (May, 1946), 235–59.

Blue buds or pitchy blooms. Be content—
Expansions, diffusions—content to be

The unspotted imbecile revery,
The heraldic center of the world

Of blue, blue sleek with a hundred chins,
The amorist Adjective aflame . . . .

The poem might be paraphrased in some such fashion as
this. The poet should be content to be at the center of his
being, which is his sensibilities and the imagination arising
therefrom. Sometimes this loyalty betrays him into writing
"pitchy blooms" rather than "blue buds," but better this
than the verses of the reasoning mind. These lines, if any
proof were needed after *Owl's Clover*, make it plain that
Stevens understands imagination to have its source not in
the "mind" but in the sensibilities.

Two of Stevens' dramatis personae who witness and pon-
der the mysterious realm of sensibility and imagination are
the rabbi and the scholar. The two have their scholarship
in common. The poet in "Le Monocle de Mon Oncle"
thinks of the nature of love first like "a dull scholar," then
like a "dark rabbi" in serious study he ponders man's limi-
tation ("a gobbet in my mincing world"), but later, having
discovered the imagination, like a "rose rabbi." In "The Sun
This March," from *Ideas of Order*, the rabbi is appealed to
as "true savant" who might be able to tell the poet about
his place in this dark world, but in "Like Decorations in a
Nigger Cemetery" the rabbi is presented as one who prevents men from discovering that their lot is solely in this
physical world. A question about the nature of symbols in
"Life on a Battleship" is referred to the rabbis for answering. The scholar, of course, has not the religious functions

of the rabbi. He has his origins, as do the poet and musician, in the "subman." He has a head bulging with speculations and with wonderment. Sometimes in his pursuit of learning he loses his animality, the "gaudium of being" known to Jocundus and "medium men." Even his final knowledge, his "metaphysics," however, is lost in the "drifting waste":

> Funest philosophers and ponderers,
> Their evocations are the speech of clouds.

The scholar is like Phosphor, another of the figures, who reads by his own light.

That Stevens tends to identify the poet and the musician is readily evident of course not only from "The Man With the Blue Guitar" but also from *Harmonium*. The titles of a number of poems, "Sad Strains of a Gay Waltz," "Mozart," "Asides on the Oboe" and "The Creation of Sound," make it equally evident. The range of instruments the poet is made to employ extends from the guitar, banjo, mandolin, marimba, hautboy, trombone, bugle, lute, zither, tambourine and tom tom to any old horn.

Stevens conceives of the poet as helping to create a world in which men are united in harmonious movements. When men discover the nature of their common desire and belief they live serenely within their myth. In our time we are witnessing the demise of a way of belief. The world that is dying is symbolized for Stevens by swans swimming peacefully on their little lakes, waltzes, and statues of men on horseback. Now it is an "old casino in the woods," boarded up and whipped by rain. When he wishes to suggest, as in "Academic Discourse at Havana," the feelings of ease and rightness with which a way of life comes into being he sees it rising out of promise to become

the sooth
Of trombones floating in the trees. . . .

Again, we are said to live

In a chiaroscuro where
One sits and plays the blue guitar.

Stevens is saying that poetry, like music, belongs to the realm of the sensibilities and imagination. The sounds made by the musician and the "sounds," a frequent metonym for poetry, made by the poet serve the same ends. It is appropriate therefore that musical instruments are prominent in the iconography of Stevens' poetical world.

The moon is also a persistent symbol of the sensibilities and imagination. In "Lunar Paraphrase" and "The Public Square," both from *Harmonium*, the moon is seen as "the mother of pathos and pity" and as looking down on us "with its porcelain leer." The moon in the final poem in *Notes toward a Supreme Fiction* is a symbol of the things of imagination. The poet

Patches the moon together in his room
To his Virgilian cadences . . . .

Sometimes, as in "Men Made Out of Words," from *Transport to Summer*, the symbolism of music is conjoined with that of the moon; and on occasion, as in "God Is Good. It is a Beautiful Night," the symbolism of color is added to that of music and the moon.

It is Stevens' conviction that the imagination, the agent of our sensibilities, has not been free to function freely. In our time, even as in Coleridge's, the rationalists have been suspicious, often contemptuous, of the realm of the sensibilities, and with it of the imagination.

Politic man
Has ordained imagination as the fateful sin.

Reality has been an honorific term, but *imagination* a pejorative. Stevens realizes the terrible irony of decrying imagination, the agent for the creation of values, in a time so desperately in need of it. And in his creation of an interrelated body of images and symbols, collectively giving evidence of "solid reality," he has demonstrated both our need for an imagined reality and the absurdity of pretending that reality has significant relationships only with rationality.

VIII

The Supreme Fictions

For Stevens the imagination is the agency that creates values. It does not follow that he believes it can create a rigorously explicit set of values. In *Owl's Clover* he questions the wisdom of attempting to live by any freshly imagined blueprint. A way of life evolves slowly, by trial. The values a people live with are affected by the conventions of their past, their surroundings, and their currently influential notions and attitudes. Men do nonetheless have a constant nature and constant needs, some of which may be lost sight of. In our time because of a few simple-minded emphases, such as the distrust of imagination, together with certain forces largely outside our control, such as the almost incessant bombardment of stimuli that disturbs our peace of mind and ease of contemplation, we seem unable to conceive and maintain images of the nobler aspects of man.

Toward the end of the famous passage in which he defined imagination Coleridge [1] said that "it struggles to idealize and to unify." He added that it is "essentially *vital*, even as all objects (*as* objects) are essentially fixed and dead." Toward the end of "The Noble Rider and the Sound of Words" there is a passage with a similar sense and import:

[1] *Biographia Literaria*, XIII.

Yet the imagination gives to everything that it touches a peculiarity, and it seems to me that the peculiarity of the
imagination is nobility, of which there are many degrees.
This inherent nobility is the source of another, which our
extremely headstrong generation regards as false and decadent. I mean that nobility which is our spiritual height
and depth. . . .

Again, in his final paragraph, Stevens echoes Coleridge's
account of objects as objects being fixed and dead:

But as a wave is a force and not the water of which it is
composed, which is never the same, so nobility is a force
and not the manifestations of which it is composed, which
are never the same.

Almost always poets have striven to discover nobility,
even though, as Stevens' remark about there being many
"degrees" of nobility implies, its expression from poem to
poem will differ. The ideal of nobility seems not unrelated
to other aspects of imagination, ordering, elevating, inten-
sifying and making purposeful the "realities" with which
it works. In listening for evidences of nobility and in strug-
gling to express them the poet is striving for the kind of
order, nobility, we find most meaningful.

For Stevens there is no contradiction involved in seeing
nobility both as a creation of the imagination and as actual,
or true. He acknowledges that it is believed in with different degrees of intensity or acceptance from age to age, or
from person to person. He has apparently felt himself under
no compulsion to label expressions of nobility unreal, or
even as "pseudo-statements," merely because many of his
contemporaries believe we can give unqualified acceptance
"only to certified scientific statements." [2] It is enough for
him that people in various societies have accepted and at-

[2] I. A. Richards, *Science and Poetry* (New York, Norton, 1926).

tempted to live with the ideal of nobility. Stevens has not found himself in the situation described by I. A. Richards in 1926:

> Countless pseudo-statements—about God, about the universe, about human nature, the relations of mind to mind, about the soul, its rank and destiny—pseudo-statements which are pivotal points in the organisation of the mind, vital to its well-being, have suddenly become, for sincere, honest and informed minds, impossible to believe. For centuries they have been believed; now they are gone, irrecoverably; and the knowledge which has killed them is not of a kind upon which an equally fine organisation of the mind can be based.

Since Richards included the statements made in *King Lear* among his pseudo-statements (statements which present us with useful attitudes but are not "true") we may assume that statements intending to express a belief in the actuality of nobility would also be called "pseudo-statements." Richards explains that pseudo-statements arise from the same source "as that from which the Magical View of the world arose." By Magical View Richards obviously means statements about God, the supernatural, the soul, nobility, and so forth. Stevens would undoubtedly agree with Richards that man's imagination alone was responsible for the Magical View. He would not find it necessary to label false or "pseudo" expressions of idealism, such as those Richards points to, merely because the imagination has been responsible for projecting certain beliefs that now seem to many to be demonstrably untrue.[3]

In stating in "The Noble Rider" that an imaginative ex-

[3] With the essential position of Richards' *Coleridge on the Imagination* (New York, Harcourt, Brace, 1935) Stevens would seem to be in close agreement. In "The Noble Rider" he refers several times to that book.

pression has the "strength of reality or none at all," Stevens
means we must accept as true or real that upon which the
imagination depends. Thus, if we do not believe in the existence of nobility, or do not believe in it with any intensity, imaginative expressions of it, as in the statue of
Bartolommeo Colleoni by the Renaissance sculptor Verrocchio, seem unreal. Stevens selected this statue as an
example because it is "on the edge of the world in which
we live today," a form magnifying us in our eyes, giving us
a sense of our potential courage and fortitude. "It seems,
nowadays, what it may very well not have seemed a few
years ago, a little overpowering, a little magnificent." We
might pose the question in another way by asking whether
we would attend with any considerable degree of belief to
a statue of a soldier contemporary with us, conceived by a
sculptor as noble or heroic. Such figures are likely to be associated in our minds with "propaganda" or unsophisticated
passion.

Stevens characterizes the statue of Andrew Jackson by
Clark Mills as a work of fancy. The parts, including Jackson's raising his hat in a gay gesture to the ladies, and the
beautiful tail of the horse, were not conceived out of any
deep need of a mind to know and realize itself, but by
choice, by easy association, in a way known to Mills' generation. "Treating this work as typical, it is obvious that the
American will as a principle of the mind's being is easily
satisfied in its efforts to realize itself in knowing itself."
There may be, he adds, works in which neither reality nor
imagination is present. But for Stevens the basic subject is
the pressure of reality against, and at the expense of,
imagination.

In the tendency of moderns like Freud to label art "illusion" he finds such a pressure. More perspicaciously, he
finds in Picasso's and Braque's concern with "the science
of painting" and Schönberg's concern with "the science of

music" the work of men who emphasize the real at the expense of the imaginative and the ideal. Stevens is not saying that there are no men of imagination in our time. He is saying that certain expressions of the imagination, like the idea of nobility, exist in art today often in diminished state or on sufferance.

All of Stevens' written comments on Eliot, Williams, Ransom, and Marianne Moore tend to emphasize their abilities to make their poetry out of materials that seem to us actual or real. He writes of the "anti-poetic," of "making a legend of reality," or of furnishing a "revelation of reality." But all genuine poets, in Stevens' term, are "romantics."

> The chatter about escapism is, to my way of thinking, merely common cant. . . . Escapism has a pejorative sense, which it cannot be supposed that I include in the sense in which I use the word. The pejorative sense applies where the poet is not attached to reality, which, for my part, I regard as fundamental.

The reality the poet sees and experiences is caught up meaningfully, and luminously, in the poet's language. "The Emperor of Ice Cream," reputedly one of his most obscure poems, exhibits the relationship between illusion and things-as-they-are. It is written in the essentially gaudy language which he says he admires.

> Call the roller of big cigars,
> The muscular one, and bid him whip
> In kitchen cups concupiscent curds.
> Let the wenches dawdle in such dress
> As they are used to wear, and let the boys
> Bring flowers in last month's newspapers.
> Let be be finale of seem.
> The only emperor is the emperor of ice-cream.

Take from the dresser of deal,
Lacking the three glass knobs, that sheet
On which she embroidered fantails once
And spread it so as to cover her face.
If her horny feet protrude, they come
To show how cold she is, and dumb.
Let the lamp affix its beam.
The only emperor is the emperor of ice-cream.

Whatever seems to be—"Let be be finale of seem"—for all
practical purposes *is*. Life is change or flux, a shifting from
illusion to reality; from delight and enjoyment—"The only
emperor is the emperor of ice-cream"—to difficult experiences. We should accept it as such. Into the context of the
poem Stevens has introduced one of the most difficult of
experiences, death. There is no blinking at the full import
of it: "If her horny feet protrude, they come/ To show
how cold she is, and dumb." She has been poor, as "the
dresser of deal/ Lacking the three glass knobs" suggests.
That is another hard reality. But she too has had her little
enjoyments—as the sheet on which "she embroidered fantails once" suggests.

Nor is there any pretense that life around her stops.
Often, as Stevens indicates, it quickens in the presence of
death. At funerals there is often a great deal of smoking—
"Call the roller of big cigars"—as well as eating and drinking—"and bid him whip/ In kitchen cups concupiscent
curds." The words "wenches" and "concupiscent" can hardly
be accidental. The former of course carries sexual connotations, and the latter, "concupiscent curds," suggests drinks
that arouse physical desires. The living, however, are not
disrespectful of the dead. They observe their rituals: sitting
with the corpse and bringing flowers wrapped, appropri-
ately "in last month's newspapers."

This is the way our lives are. So be it—"Let the lamp

affix its beam." We should not only accept it but we should understand it: "The only emperor is the emperor of ice-cream."

This same employment of the harsh reality or the ugly transformed by the imagination is found in "Le Monocle de Mon Oncle": [4]

> Last night, we sat beside a pool of pink,
> Clippered with lilies scudding the bright chromes,
> Keen to the point of starlight, while a frog
> Boomed from his very belly odious chords.

In this poem he raises the question, as he does elsewhere, of the relation of sex to love:

>   I pursued,
>   And still pursue, the origin and course
>   Of love.

His studies, it would seem, have convinced him that love is indebted to the idealizing power of the imagination. It arises out of the affective side of our beings. In "Men Made Out of Words," from *Transport to Summer*, he asks,

> What should we be without the sexual myth,
> The human revery or poem of death?

Similarly the hero owes his existence to our and his sensibilities, to the idealizing imagination. The prisoner in "Montrachet-le-Jardin," from *Parts of a World*, is a "salty skeleton" who "Sings of an heroic world beyond the cell." We always have had and still need the "rhetorics" that accept and teach heroism:

[4] Alfred Kreymborg in *Our Singing Strength* points out Stevens' indebtedness to "En Monocle" by Donald Evans, a pre-World War I esthete whose work shows the influence of the British nineties and the French symbolists.

Man must become the hero of his world.

"Examination of the Hero in a Time of War," a long poem, is the fullest account or examination Stevens gives to the subject. In Section VI he asks,

> Unless we believe in the hero, what is there
> To believe?

Can we, he asks again in another section, feed only our bellies, "live on dry descriptions," and "crumbs of whimsy?" We need heroism as we need love:

>   The hero
> Glides to his meeting like a lover
> Mumbling a secret, passionate message.

The hero is no individual man, nor is he the icon, the "marble soiled by pigeons"—"He is a feeling," not an image. He is whatever made him—a nation, the common man, or a higher self. Seeing and conceiving him, we may be

>   capable
> Of his brave quickenings.

The hero is, if one will, a result of what in *Notes toward a Supreme Fiction*, Stevens calls the "romantic intoning." He comes alive not through "reason's click-clack" but through the idealizing imagination. Yet

> How simply the fictive hero becomes the real;
> How gladly with proper words the soldier dies,
> If he must, or lives on the bread of faithful speech.

Heroism is no more unreal, no more a "figment of the imagination" than is nobility or love. What Stevens wrote about nobility at the end of "The Noble Rider" applies to all three: None of them is

> an artifice that the mind has added to human nature. The mind has added nothing to human nature. It is a violence from within that protects us from a violence without. It is the imagination pressing back against the pressure of reality. It seems, in the last analysis, to have something to do with our self-preservation; and that, no doubt, is why the expression of it, the sound of its words, helps us to live our lives.

IX

The Poems of Our Climate

W. H. AUDEN in attempting to explain the side of Yeats that is "summed up in *A Vision*," the side of Yeats that was attracted to Celtic mythology, mediums, and occult symbolism, has said that we must consider the generation in which Yeats grew up. It was a generation which witnessed and took part in the conflict "between the Religion of Reason and the Religion of Imagination, objective truth and subjective truth, the Universal and the Individual." Auden adds that "Reason, Science, the general, seemed to be winning and Imagination, Art and the individual on the defensive." Our situation is a little different. "The true natural sciences like physics and chemistry no longer claim to explain the meaning of life." Only the so-called Social Sciences with something less than limited success claim to do that. The ground of the argument is no longer

> between Reason and Imagination but between the good and evil will, not between objectivity and subjectivity but between the integration of thought and feeling and their dissociation, not between the individual and the masses but between the social person and the impersonal state.

. . . .

In other words, the view of experience toward which Yeats was instinctively attracted (after ridding itself of some of the excesses the conflict occasioned in those who opposed the overemphasis on Reason, Objectivity and the Universal) has been more widely accepted. Poets like Yeats and Stevens, in somewhat different ways, have been effective agents in causing their later contemporaries to recognize the dangers inherent in holding to a dichotomy of thought and sensibility or objectivity and subjectivity.

Stevens asks in *The Man With the Blue Guitar,* XXII, whether the world of objectivity (things-as-they-are) really can be kept separate from our world of the sensibility (things-as-they-are-made-upon-the-blue-guitar).

> Poetry is the subject of the poem,
> From this the poem issues and
>
> To this returns. Between the two,
> Between issue and return, there is
>
> An absence in reality,
> Things as they are. Or so we say.
>
> But are these separate? Is it
> An absence for the poem, which acquires
>
> Its true appearances there, sun's green,
> Cloud's red, earth feeling, sky that thinks.
>
> From these it takes. Perhaps it gives,
> In the universal intercourse.

Both men, Yeats and Stevens, again in somewhat different ways, have written their poetry not only about the danger but the actual consequences of a society living with the dichotomy. Among the consequences has been the effect upon the writing of the poetry we call modern.

In "Bantams in Pine-Woods," from *Harmonium*, Stevens
has written intelligently and wittily about "the Universal
and the Individual." (As an example of Stevens' genius as
a rhetorician, the poem demands careful study.)

> Chieftain Iffucan of Azcan in caftan
> Of tan with henna hackles, halt!
>
> Damned universal cock, as if the sun
> Was blackamoor to bear your blazing tail.
>
> Fat! Fat! Fat! Fat! I am the personal.
> Your world is you. I am my world.
>
> You ten-foot poet among inchlings. Fat!
> Begone! An inchling bristles in these pines,
>
> Bristles, and points their Appalachian tangs,
> And fears not portly Azcan nor his hoos.

We are all bantams, all inchlings, but some bantams would
demean the personal and the local and elevate only the universal and the general. Whom, among the latter, does he
have in mind? Probably all who are uncritical proponents
of "objective truth" as opposed to "subjective truth," those
with minds like Thomas Huxley's who for a time at least
forced those with minds like Yeats' to retreat or to fight
merely a rearguard action. Probably, too, those among the
poets who aspire to be Olympian, to rise above their role as
human inchlings. The poets who use a grandiose rhetoric,
who forget that their world, like ours, is personal. The objective is meaningful only in terms of the subjective. The
universal is conceivable only in relation to the particular.
Stevens, employing the symbol of the "universal cock," is

ridiculing the pretentiousness of those who have set up the false antitheses and insisted that they be accepted.

Despite his ridicule of exaggerated rhetoric, of "hoos," Stevens appreciates the power of language. The Yokel in "The Plot Against the Giant," from *Harmonium*, is undone not by the odor of flowers nor by beautifully colored cloths but by language, by

> Heavenly labials in a world of gutturals.

Years later, in "Academic Discourse at Havana," from *Ideas of Order*, there are further notes on the function of the poet. He may, through his rarities and harmonies, "reconcile us to ourselves." The night may be still and it may be meaningless

> But let the poet on his balcony
> Speak and the sleepers in their sleep shall move.

Poetry, he wrote in *The Man With the Blue Guitar*, XXIV, is a means to knowledge, even to desperate knowledge. Later still, in "Poetry Is a Destructive Force," from *Parts of a World*, he expressed the same appreciation. It is a strength within one comparable to possessing the strength of a lion or an ox. It is a mistake to think that rhetoric never makes anything happen:

> The lion sleeps in the sun
> Its nose on its paws
> It can kill a man.

It is by metaphor, he writes in "Poem Written at Morning," from *Parts of a World*, that rhetoric is made possible. It is a loose way of speaking to say we "see"; it were better to say we "experience." And we experience through metaphor.

> Thus, the pineapple was a leather fruit,
> A fruit for pewter, thorned and palmed. . . .

Stevens' most intense examination of metaphor was reserved for his prose study in *Three Academic Pieces*. But Stevens is also concerned, as is evident from the first section of *Notes toward a Supreme Fiction*, to present a sense of real objects as they exist as primary sense experiences.

> Our sense of these things changes and they
> change,
> Not as in metaphor, but in our sense
> Of them.[1]

Even though Stevens lays great stress on bringing objects alive, making them radiant through metaphor, he also recognizes that some objects live in our senses, in responses that are not or cannot be articulated. It is as though the meanings are too thick or too numerous for articulation. This puts them "beyond the rhetorician's touch."

The creators and critics of modern poetry have concerned themselves with the place of meaning in poetry. Eliot, for example, has said that for one kind of reader "meaning" serves to keep the "mind diverted and quiet, while the poem does its work . . . much as the imaginary burglar is always provided with a bit of nice meat for the house dog." And Yeats somewhere observed that in the best folk poetry there is a curious absence of explicit, exact meaning. There is, in other words, an awareness that poetry works not, to

[1] This quotation is from "Bouquet of Roses in Sunlight," *Poetry: A Magazine of Verse*, LXXI (Oct., 1947), 11. Although subsequent to *Notes toward a Supreme Fiction*, it illustrates the point discussed here more neatly than any of the poems in the earlier sequence.

use Stevens' term, with "radiant reason" alone but works also with the murky parts of experience and of the mind. It is not surprising, therefore, to find two poems in *Transport to Summer* that treat this matter. In "Man Carrying Thing" we read:

> The poem must resist the intelligence
> Almost successfully.

And in "The Creation of Sound" he criticizes a poet, X, because his poems

>   do not make the visible a little hard
> To see.

Several of the poems in *Ideas of Order* express an awareness that our contemporaries, for the most part, have little faith in the value of poetry. In Section XXXII of "Like Decorations in a Nigger Cemetery" Stevens admits poetry lives "uncertainly" but he adds that it lives "radiantly beyond much lustier blurs." The poet in "Academic Discourse at Havana" is seen as a "part of nature," and as a "part of us." How shortsighted or how ridiculous it is, then, to attack the poet or to dismiss poetry. Yet, in "Mozart, 1935" he gives one of the reasons for the attacks. There are immediate problems of an economic and social nature:

> It is because they carry down the stairs
> A body in rags.

Even though they throw stones on his roof, the poet, Stevens adds, should learn his art that he may be the voice by which the "sorrow is released." Despite feeling obliged to give such advice, he does confess, in "Sailing After Lunch," that it "hurts" to hear the word "poetry" or, more specifically, the word "romantic" treated as a *"pejorative."* The preoccupation we have had with the delimited fact is a delusion. It has made us giddy.

"Of Modern Poetry," from *Parts of a World,* epitomizes the problems of the poet in an Alexandrian world. These problems, of course, have been treated elsewhere, perhaps most clearly by Yeats and Eliot. Put in one set of terms, they are the problems of attempting to write in a time that has no universally acceptable system of belief and corresponding body of cultural symbols. The poet is obliged not only to discover but to be sure of his belief, to justify it for his reader, and to express it in symbols that are understandable and affecting. Once, Stevens says, "the scene was set" and the poet "repeated what Was in the script." Now he must construct his own stage (as, indeed, Stevens himself has done, in terms of a subject matter, beliefs, a dramatis personae and an iconography peculiar to his poetry), and he must write for an extremely self-conscious audience, for an audience that listens

Not to the play, but to itself. . . .

In "The Poems of Our Climate," from the same volume, he treats a subject that may be considered an aspect and a consequence of the cultural situation treated in "Of Modern Poetry." In it he says that the ideal of simplicity, of describing natural objects, however beautifully done, is not enough. There always remains "the never resting mind." The mind itself wants to create. It has its own criteria. Among them, surprisingly, is its liking for the imperfect, for the "flawed words and stubborn sounds."

Stevens' autobiographical "The Comedian as the Letter C" is a history of the development of his understanding of the nature of poetry and the poet's role in society. The poet, viewed as a valet-comedian, although certainly not as a ridiculous or unwitting one, moves from a highly personal romanticism through, first, a stark, then an exotic realism, to a realism that means for him accepting the world on its own terms and viewing experience both indulgently and skeptically. It is an account of a voyage between the "sun," the objective world, and the "moon," the subjective world. The "pith" of the poem is summed up in a little fable:

> The world, a turnip once so readily plucked.
> Sacked up and carried overseas, daubed out
> Of its ancient purple, pruned to the fertile main,
> And sown again by the stiffest realist,
> Came reproduced in purple, family font,
> The same insoluble lump. The fatalist
> Stepped in and dropped the chuckling down his craw,
> Without grace or grumble.

In this poem the emphasis is on "things-as-they-are."

> For realists what is is what should be.

Usually Stevens presents reality in a larger or at least in a different perspective, as composed both of things-as-they-are *and* the things of the imagination.

Poetry as the agency that elevates experiences as well as ideals is touched on in "A Pastoral Nun."

> She said poetry and apotheosis are one.

In the realm of religion, it is implied, apotheosis gives radiance and rapture to human experience. Through poetry these same experiences typified by "morning," "summer," "night," and "the hero" (in addition to other symbols from the mythology of Stevens' own poetry) are not merely humanized but made to live in "an immense activity."

A somewhat similar point is touched upon in poem III of the first section of *Notes toward a Supreme Fiction.* "The poem refreshes life. . . ." It is a means of making us see, with a candor and freshness, as though the world were new and we could view it newly. And in poem IX from the second section he says the language the poet uses ranges from the common speech, the "vulgate," to the "imagination's Latin." To be strong the poet's peculiar language must be compounded with the "peculiar potency of the general." Throughout *Notes toward a Supreme Fiction* he implies that poetry should play an important role in the fictions necessary to transform and humanize the world.

X

Resemblances and Precision

THE DOCTRINE of "correspondences," a term with many
meanings and covering a broad range of experiences, finds a
place in Stevens' poetry. It would seem that this doctrine
arose from a sense of the need to express relationships between the world of matter and spirit. It gave rise to the attempt to translate one sense impression into another. For
Stevens the doctrine of correspondences is included in his
concern with the realm of resemblances, with the ability of
the imagination to see resemblances between things. With
other poets who write in the Symbolist tradition, Stevens appears to be indebted to Baudelaire's "Correspondances":

> Nature is a temple where living pillars
> Let sometimes emerge confused words;
> Man comes there over forests of symbols
> Which watch him with intimate eyes.
>
> Like those deep echoes that meet from afar
> In a dark and profound harmony,
> As vast as night and clarity,
> So perfumes, colours, tones answer each other. . . .[1]

[1] Translated by Geoffrey Wagner, *Flowers of Evil* (New York, New
Directions, 1946). It may be observed that one of Stevens' frequently

But Stevens does not seem to have appropriated Baudelaire's belief that spirituality or beauty or truth, existing in some objective though hidden realm, is to be caught by the poet in his material symbols. Stevens is deeply concerned with the ideal, but for him it is to be found in the individual's imagination, not in some transcendental or Platonic realm of Ideas. The poet can create a unity, draw seemingly divergent things together, but he is working from within his own mind. "Connoisseur in Chaos" indicates that Stevens does not believe that all "things partake of one." That

> was the theory, when bishops' books
> Resolved the world. We cannot go back to that.

Baudelaire's belief in this unity gave rise to his theory, which has been neatly expressed by Enid Starkie, of the relationship among the arts.

> Since art in its totality reflects a vision, then each art—painting, music, sculpture and poetry—expresses in its own language, using its own hieroglyphics, what it has perceived in the realm where there are no boundaries, in the realm of pure beauty and truth. It follows thence that it matters little which artistic language is used to express the spiritual experience. Baudelaire imagined that it might be possible to find one art which would comprise all the languages, would appeal to all his senses "fondus en un." In his poetry he endeavoured to use the idiom of all the arts, to render what his eye saw not merely in line and colour, what his ear perceived not only in harmony, but to glide imperceptibly from one mode of expression to the other. Since "les parfums, les couleurs et les sons se repondent" then he could render colour by means of harmony and sound by means of colour and line.[2]

---

used symbols, the "hautboy," or oboe, is used by Baudelaire in this poem. And Baudelaire's "Harmonie du Soir" may have suggested Stevens' title *Harmonium*.

[2] *Ibid.*, p. 8.

Stevens' symbolist esthetic includes the translating of one sense impression into another. Poetry is identified with "sound," "music," or painting, an idea merges with a color, a thought with an odor or perfume. Presumably he believes that synesthesia is a fact of the mind which should be recognized and given its place in the language of poetry. Taken together, all the arts suggest a common concern, a reaching toward the ideal that each individually expresses in a fragmentary way. Perhaps the most notable examples of "correspondences" in Stevens' poetry are in "Peter Quince at the Clavier":

> Thinking of your blue-shadowed silk,
> Is music. It is like the strain
> Waked in the elders by Susanna.

Again,

> Susanna's music touched the bawdy strings
> Of those white elders; but, escaping,
> Left only Death's ironic scraping.
> Now, in its immortality, it plays
> On the clear viol of her memory,
> And makes a constant sacrament of praise.

Sprinkled through volumes subsequent to *Harmonium* are lines like these: "Whose green mind bulges with complicated hues," "Cinerarias have a speaking sheen," "Like rhetoric in a narration of the eye," "To drone the green phrases of its juvenal," and "Reddens the sand with its red-coloured noise." Liadoff's "epitones" are "the colors of the air," and voices of the wind "Are sounds blown by a blower into shapes."

Stevens' concern with resemblances, then, is much broader than his awareness of synesthesia, the merging of one art with another or even with the fact that each art in its way presses toward an expression of the ideal. His larger awareness, which at center is a concern with metaphor, he has discussed in "The Realm of Resemblances," the essay in *Three Academic Pieces*. A poetic metaphor, he says, "appears to be poetry at its source. It is. At least it is poetry at one of its sources although not necessarily its most fecundating." The realm of resemblance also includes that of ambiguity, which in turn includes that of connotation.

Stevens thinks of poetry as a means of satisfying a desire for seeing resemblance. In the "act of satisfying the desire for resemblance, it enhances the sense of reality, heightens it, intensifies it." In the third section of the poem "Someone Puts a Pineapple Together," he gives an example of the way in which the imagination may "extend" an object. Once his imagination is free to play around the pineapple sitting on the table the pineapple *becomes:*

1. The hut stands by itself beneath the palms.
2. Out of their bottle the green genii come.
3. A vine has climbed the other side of the wall.

4. The sea is spouting upward out of rocks.
5. Symbol of feasts and of oblivion.
6. White sky, pink sun, trees on a distant peak.

7. These lozenges are nailed-up lattices.
8. The owl sits humped. It has a hundred eyes.
9. The coconut and cockerel in one.

10. This is how yesterday's volcano looks.
11. There is an island Palahude by name—
12. An uncivil shape like a gigantic haw.

Not all of these resemblances are equally good. Stevens admits that "between resemblances one is always a little

more perfect than another." But it is a considerable feat
merely to conceive twelve images which resemble a pineapple. It is an achievement frequently repeated in Stevens'
poetry.

In the same essay he mentions resemblance between two
dissimilar things. It "complements and reinforces that which
the two dissimilar things have in common. It makes it brilliant." If the things compared are in most respects unlike
we think of the comparison as a conceit, in Samuel John-
son's terms "a kind of *discordia concors*; a combination of
dissimilar images, or discovery of occult resemblances in
things apparently unlike." The conceit is commonly thought
of as being of two kinds, condensed and expanded. Of the
former we may instance two from *Owl's Clover*:

> The future must bear within it every past,
> Not least the pasts destroyed, magniloquent
> Syllables, pewter on ebony.

and

> The envoi to the past
> Is largely another winding of the clock.

Of the latter, the extended conceit, we may instance such
poems as "Bantams in Pine-Woods," "The Bird With the
Coppery Keen Claws," "Peter Quince at the Clavier," "Stars
at Tallapoosa," "A High Toned Old Christian Woman,"
and others both in *Harmonium* and the later volumes. The
first few lines of "Of Hartford In a Purple Light" suggest
the wit and the manner Stevens can employ in probing
and expanding a conceit:

> A long time you have been making the trip
> From Havre to Hartford, Master Soleil,
> Bringing the lights of Norway and all that.

A long time the ocean has come with you,
Shaking the water off, like a poodle,
That splatters incessant thousands of drops,

Each drop a petty tricolor.

Only a highly imaginative poet could perceive the little
cluster of related resemblances necessary to the creating of
such a conceit. Stevens creates them often and with apparent ease. A similar ease is evident in his manipulation of
imagery, symbol and statement in the service of ambiguity,
"so favorable to the poetic mind," and connotation. Both
are based on resemblance, and both intensify our pleasure
in and awareness of reality.

Commenting on interpretations, printed in *The Explicator*, of "The Emperor of Ice Cream," Stevens said that
works having their "origin in the imagination or in the
emotions (poems)" have ambiguous meanings rather than
a single rational meaning. Usually the meanings, caught in
an imagery giving concrete and dramatic force to the theme
or introductory statement, are readily perceivable. And frequently as in these lines from "Le Monocle de Mon Oncle"
the imagery is composed of enough specific detail to make
the statement not merely complex but convincing:

> For me, the firefly's quick, electric stroke
> Ticks tediously the time of one more year.
> And you? Remember how the crickets came
> Out of their mother grass, like little kin,
> In the pale nights, when your first imagery
> Found inklings of your bond to all that dust.

The flicks of light cast by the firefly are regular and brief,
suggesting the ticking off of years, after which for us there
will be no more light at all. The crickets, our kin, share the

summer nights, and, dust like us, have their life from the
earth. The nights are "pale," beautiful, but as mysterious as
our lives. The poet probing his images finds "inklings"
(surely an intentional pun), new ways of saying and of
carrying profound conviction of our being dust. Perhaps
"complex" is not quite the right word for this kind of
imagery. It is an imagery in which significant detail from
the physical world serves a theme and arouses connotations and overtones that live strongly in our sensibilities. In Stevens' poetry, as Joubert would have all
poetry, "each word reverberates like the note of a well tuned
lyre, and always leaves behind it a multitude of vibra-
tions." [3]

Stevens' usual, or at least very frequent, method in writing a poem is to make a general initial statement. Thus in
one of the sections of *Notes toward a Supreme Fiction*:

> Two things of opposite nature seem to depend
> On one another, as a man depends
> On a woman, day on night, the imagined
> On the real. This is the origin of change.

Usually, too, the statement is elaborated, qualified, enlarged,
and probed. And all the while, there is being evoked, as
well, by means of metaphor, variant phrases, and the employment of deftly appropriate rhythms, a conviction or
strong sense of the experience generalized about in the introductory abstraction. In "Fabliau of Florida," from *Harmonium*, the generalization is held until the final couplet.
The couplet is not quite abstract and is therefore hardly
typical, but the method of the poem is indicative of much
else that is characteristic of his method.

[3] Stevens is sometimes credited with having influenced Hart Crane. A
fairly good case might be made showing similarities between the diction
of "Le Monocle de Mon Oncle" and some of the poems in *The White
Buildings*. This is also true of "Sea Surface Full of Clouds."

Barque of phosphor
On the palmy beach,

Move outward into heaven
Into the alabasters
And night blues.

Foam and cloud are one.
Sultry moon monsters
Are dissolving

Fill your black hull
With white moonlight

There will never be an end
To this droning of the surf.

The "statement," there will never be an answer to the mystery in which we live, is clear enough. The roaring of the sea, the dissolving clouds, and the firmament extend the simple "statement," giving us as it were convincing and moving proof. Because we are in and a part of this world we should accept it in its fullness—live lives of the sensibilities and imagination. The language itself is both ambiguous and suggestive. The barque could be *poetry* or *a human being*. The luminous barque floats on a dark sea; the beach is rich with physical life; the sky is beautiful with brilliantly contrasting "alabaster" and "night blue," the alabaster repeating the whiteness of "phosphor" and preparing for the whiteness and suggestions thereof in "foam," "cloud," "moonlight," and surf, and the symbolism of blue and moonlight signifying the realm of sensibility and imagination which the poet would not have us neglect or deny. The repetitive use of dark and light shades supports, after the poet's subtly evocative way, the statement. There is no attempt to bludgeon the reader into acceptance. The lines are delivered deftly, with adequate but not excessive care to bind the phrases alliteratively. The abstraction or generalization made by a poet like Stevens, capable of seeing and evoking both the feelings appropriate to a statement and the qualifications called for, will rarely if ever sound fatuous.

On occasion, however, the abstractions lack the power to arouse our feelings. One finds such lines more often in the later poems, as in *Esthétique du Mal* or *A Primitive like an Orb*. Again, there are poems in which the repetitions support not merely a tenuous but a vague and unrealized rather than a subtly elaborated subject matter. In "Chocorua To Its Neighbor," from *Transport to Summer*, one may read with the sense that a subject is being made ready to declare itself, that the hints and suggestions are building toward a center but finally come to recognize that the poem says in a realized way in the first few stanzas all that is to be said. "Repetitions of a Young Captain" exhibits, on a lesser scale, some of the same weaknesses.

It would seem, in regard to some of the later poems, that both the verse form, the unrhymed three lined stanzas, suitable to expository writing, and the generalized themes, such as the finding of a center in various experiences, invite both overextension and an element of vagueness. And it could be that Stevens' own successes with language, weaving a pattern, teasing a world of poetry out of his own sensibilities and insights, have betrayed him into themes and subjects that remain, perhaps must remain, intransigent.

Stevens is aware, as his concern that we perceive the limitations of the strict rationalists implies, of the need for the poet to understand the faculties serving our affective sides; but he is also aware of the need for abstractions. Stevens' technique of using generalized statements to introduce, to conclude, or to epitomize a theme is not his only use of abstract terms.

Fairly often he combines an abstract or essentially abstract term with a concrete term. We find this device in such phrases as these: "metaphysical pine," "green flauntings," "calico idea," "granite monotony," "sexual blossoms," "ruddy pulses," "mottled mood," "brilliant mercy," "cloud of sleep," "swollen [w]ith thought," "final slate," "dark italics," "milky millions," and so on. One of the effects of the device is that we feel ourselves in an intellectual realm in which our sensibilities are quickened.

Does Stevens' employment of generalized statements and elaborations of his stated themes imply that he is a *ruminative* poet? Do his thoughts engender a kind of passivity in which one line or word is associated somewhat loosely with another? If we say, for example, that he is not strictly in the tradition of modernist poets who would create a language in which the images and symbols themselves, rather than generally abstract statements carry the meaning, does it follow that he, like Wordsworth, say, reports his feelings ("And I have felt A presence that disturbs me with the joy of elevated thought . . .")? In other words, if Stevens is not employing the manner we associate with the early Eliot or the manner we associate with Wordsworth, what manner precisely is he employing? By and large, as indicated above, he makes a general statement, then proceeds to evoke a fuller sense of it, not merely by imagery but by paradox, puns, antithesis, ambiguity, or direct statement. He states his ideal, and by implication his own method, in "Adult Epigram," from *Transport to Summer:*

> The romance of the precise is not the elision
> Of the tired romance of imprecision . . . .

A word in one of Stevens' lines, when he is writing at his best, is precise and significant. It catches his meaning exactly and in an effective language. Three lines from a poem examined earlier, "The Bird With the Coppery Keen Claws," exhibits this manner. Stevens' world is budding, ripeness, and death. Man participates in it, but because he has a sense of possessing "pure intellect" discovers ultimate meanings "in the wilderness." Stevens describes the world, color, the sun, eating, the sense of knowing, and so forth. The description of the bird is delusively simple:

> Above the forest of the parakeets
> A parakeet of parakeets prevails,
> A pip of life amid a mort of tails.

As soon as we suspect the literal meaning is not all, the underlying meaning suggests itself, detail by detail. Why parakeet instead of parrot? Because parakeet suggests Paraclete. Why "forest of the parakeets"? Because men make God in the image of man. Why parakeet and not some other colorful bird? Because the parakeet speaks, and speech is the source of our delusion of understanding the meaning of the universe. Why "parakeet of parakeets"? Because of the echo it suggests with King of Kings, or Lord of Lords. Why "mort of tails" instead of many tails? Because mort is a pun on death and relates to the ironic commentary on our sense of understanding the meaning of death treated in the first two lines. The language fits the world he is describing and the commentary he is implying.

The paradox is frequent in Stevens' poetry. It is quite likely to occur when he is treating his key subject, the nature of imagination:

> The imagination, the one reality
> In this imagined world.

Or in such instances as these: "My hands such sharp, imagined things," "Pleased that the irrational is rational," "I taste at the root of my tongue the unreal of what is real," "in the dry machine Of ocean," and "It was evening all afternoon." Stevens has been quoted earlier as saying that metaphor is poetry at one of its sources. The language of indirection, which includes paradox, as well as metaphor, is also poetry at one of its sources. Given his subject, about which his contemporaries have many preconceptions which he does not share, Stevens has found in paradox an instrument for impact and shock as well as brevity and precision.

Stevens' strong belief that man is the luminous intelligence of this world, surrounded by a mysterious nothingness, causes him to reach out for a kind of paradox that involves ideas of negation and nothingness.[4] One must, he wrote in "The Snow Man," have "a mind of winter" to be able to contemplate a winter scene without depression or despair. The wind blows

> For the listener, who listens in the snow,
> And, nothing himself, beholds
> Nothing that is not there and the nothing that is.

Such figures apparently grow out of a striving to express a feeling that seems beyond the capacity of ordinary speech to capture. They carry metaphysical implications, as does Donne's

> But I am by her death (which word wrongs her)
> Of the first Nothing, the elixir grown . . . .

In "Cortège for Rosenbloom" there are "infants of nothingness" and in "Of Heaven Considered as a Tomb" there is a "spiritous passage into nothingness."

[4] Hi Simons finds these figures an indication of Stevens' debt to Mallarmé.

The imagination creates a seeming order out of a universe without human meaning. In *Owl's Clover* the poet brings "down from nowhere nothing's wax-like blooms." Ananke is described thus:

> He sees but not by sight
> He does not hear by sound.

The abstract conceptions of man, not individual men, are characterized as

> evasions like a repeated phrase,
> Which, by its repetition, comes to bear
> A meaning without a meaning.

In "Montrachet-le-Jardin" there are these phrases: "a senseless syllable," "players of aphonies," and "sounds resembling sounds." And in *Notes toward a Supreme Fiction* the poet is advised to create and perfect delicate imaginings, as delicate as "iris frettings on the blank." The paradoxical figures employing the idea of negation or employing a negative to suggest the inexpressible indicate both Stevens' view of man's place in the universe and his concern as an artist to achieve the most delicate precision of statement possible.

Another aspect of Stevens' poetic language is its uncommon but precisely employed diction. As often as not the words seem a little precious, words like *brune, milleman, wiggy, versicolorings, exhumo, seigneur, effendi, bandeaux, selvages, fortelleze, semblables, paisant, panache, princox; funest, cosseted, carked, lacustrine, prinks, coign, fubbed, coulisse, umber, anonymids, clickering,* and so forth. Some of them, of course, are from Latin and the Romance languages. All of them suggest the tone of much of the poetry. In the fourth section of "Sea Surface Full of Clouds" there

is an excellent example of Stevens' somewhat specialized
diction and his manner of controlling it.

> In that November off Tehuantepec
> The night-long slopping of the sea grew still.
> A mallow morning dozed upon the deck
>
> And made one think of musky chocolate
> And frail umbrellas. A too-fluent green
> Suggested malice in the dry machine
>
> Of ocean, pondering dank stratagem.
> Who then beheld the figures of the clouds
> Like blooms secluded in the thick marine?
>
> Like blooms? Like damasks that were shaken off
> From the loosed girdles in the spangling must.
> C'était ma foi, la nonchalance divine.
>
> The nakedness would rise and suddenly turn
> Salt masks of beard and mouths of bellowing,
> Would—But more suddenly the heaven rolled
>
> Its bluest sea-clouds in the thinking green,
> And the nakedness became the broadest blooms,
> Mile-mallows that a mallow sun cajoled.

One of the key words is *mallow*. There are groups of
connotation on two levels, one group being the associations
with the mallow family of herbs—okra, hollyhock, rose mallow, the other being those with marshmallow, the candy
formerly made from the roots of the marshmallow. There
is obviously a cluster of associations: warmth, sweetness,
muted colors, and undoubtedly there is a suggestion of sticki-
ness both from the candy and the stalks of the mallow
plants. Thus the "mallow morning" readily suggests the

"musky chocolate" in which a marshmallow might float.
The mild warmth of the morning suggests both the comfort of dozing on deck and sitting under umbrellas drinking
chocolate. There is no new reference to mallow until the
final line, "Mile mallows" and "mallow sun." The two
phrases out of the context would be almost meaningless.
Prepared for by the preceding lines they mean of course
the smooth surfaces of the ocean on a mild, warm morning. The colors in the water and in the air are muted, like
the colors of the mallow flowers. Perhaps too there is the
suggestion that the "mallow sun" helps to mute, to cajole,
the glitter and the rolling blooms in the water. Again the
word "must" is dependent upon much that precedes it. The
word signifies both intense sexual excitement and an im-
perative. And it echoes the musk of "musky chocolate."
The words around it, "damask," "loosed girdles" and "spangling" also have sexual connotations. Damask, a yellowish
white linen, is suggested by the white glimmering surface
of the water, but it in turn suggests a linen garb, especially
in this context. And "spangling" supports both the notion
of sexual excitement and the glimmering of lights on the
surface of the water. That "must" is being used in this
sense is evident from the "nakedness" that follows. Suddenly the excitement ceases and the ease suggested by the
little cluster of meanings around "mallow" is reasserted. But
the new ease is a kind that follows excitement and experience. It is an ease of a different, even a mellow, kind.
There is an ambiguity running through the lines, but each
connotation when sought out and stated can be seen to be
relevant to the passage it participates in and enriches.

The theme running through the poem is the power of
the imagination, properly stimulated, to transform a given
subject. In this instance it is the surface of the sea which
arouses various associations in the poet's mind. In Section
IV the changing surface suggests the movement from ease

to excitement to ease, in language at once evocative as description and suggestive of a similar pattern of movement in sexual relations. The tone common to Stevens' poetry, a kind of intellectualized elegance, urbane and perceptive, is here. This tone would seem to have its origin in the various techniques employed in the passage: the growth in meaningfulness of a given word as with "mallow"; the unusualness of the diction, as with "must"; the intellectuality of the manner, as with the use of the paradoxical phrase, "dry machine"; the shifting from image to image and statement to statement through the ability to perceive resemblances, as when the sea suddenly becomes feminine; the physical world in its shifting colors; the décor of an elegant world, as with a sea voyage, the sipping of chocolate under frail umbrellas, and the employment of French phrasing; the almost imperceptible use of two related sounds, *m* and *n*, which set up a kind of undercurrent of humming throughout the passage; and the slightly stressed, irregular rhyming. The passage is not fully representative, granting even the differences that would be inevitable with a different subject matter, of Stevens' manner and tone. The metrical pattern has greater regularity than usual.[5] And the passage does not suggest the degree to which the ironic manner is common to Stevens. Nor does it adequately suggest either the degree of his concern with an "anti-poetic" subject matter and imagery or his offhand casual manner.

Stevens' tone is necessarily ironic. In his view of the world and man's role there is no blinking at the difficulties or harsh realities. His "A High-Toned Old Christian Woman" or "The Bird With the Coppery Keen Claws" are ironic views of attempts to make our role more meaningful and hopeful than Stevens believes it is. He sees us, the only

[5] See Yvor Winters, *In Defense of Reason* (New York, Swallow-Morrow, 1947), pp. 103–4. This passage in Winters' study of metrics affords an excellent example of the "freedom" of Stevens' "free verse."

intelligence of this world, caught in the flux and constant change. Irony is a kind of guaranty against excesses, against exaggerated rhetoric, sentimentality or empty assertions. Stevens' irony is a mode of analysis, facile, perceptive and witty. There is a good deal of self-mockery evident in the titles of his poems, as though he were guarding against taking his own assertions too seriously. In "The Comedian as the Letter C" [6] the poet assumes the role of a valet-comedian, a mild and questioning figure. He is the "merest minuscule," the single letter of a word, and in no danger of seeing the poet as a great tragic figure wandering the wastes of this world. The Crispin of French drama, as the Crispin of *Le Legataire universel* (1708) by Jean-François Regnard, seems to be the model for Crispin, the valet-comedian of Stevens' long poem. Stevens' Crispin, like Regnard's, is caught in the irony of fortune. Stevens' Crispin comes to terms with the quotidian, not only as a man but as a poet.

> What is one man among so many men?
> What are so many men in such a world?

He will continue, however, to write his poetry, his couplet yearly. This statement has not prevented Stevens from pursuing the important themes, love, heroism, nobility. On the other hand, he is in no danger of a single-minded commitment to a romantic or tragic view:

> Crispin in one laconic phrase laid bare
> His cloudy drift and planned a colony.
> Exit the mental moonlight, exit lex,
> Rex and principium, exit the whole
> Shebang.

[6] See Hi Simons, "The Comedian as the Letter C," *The Southern Review*, V (1940), 453–68; and R. P. Blackmur, "Examples of Wallace Stevens," *The Double Agent* (New York, Arrow Editions, 1935), pp. 63–102.

Stevens' irony helps hold him close to the natural. There is an easy casualness even in his elegance. In commenting on the virtue of naturalness in poetry, Marianne Moore once wrote: "Even elate and fearsome rightness like Shakespeare's is only preserved from the offense of being 'poetic,' by his well-nested effects of helpless naturalness." Stevens' "elate and fearsome rightness" is also protected by a feeling for the genuine, the natural:

> This trivial trope reveals a way of truth.
> Our bloom is gone. We are the fruit thereof.
> Two golden gourds distended on our vines,
> Into the autumn weather, splashed with frost,
> Distorted by hale fatness, turned grotesque.
> We hang like warty squashes, streaked and rayed,
> The laughing sky will see the two of us
> Washed into rinds by rotting winter rains.

Stevens has the sense for the precise word or phrase as well as the sensibility and imagination necessary to creating the radiant atmosphere in which the commonplace and the real can be seen freshly and newly. "The morality of the poet's radiant and productive atmosphere," he has said, "is the morality of the right sensation." Stevens himself has in great abundance, to the point of genius, the powers he ascribes to the poet of creating "a truth that cannot be arrived at by the reason alone, a truth that the poet recognizes by sensation."

BIBLIOGRAPHY

I. The Poetry of Wallace Stevens

Harmonium. New York, Alfred A. Knopf, 1923.
Harmonium. New York, Alfred A. Knopf, 1931. Contains additional poems.
Ideas of Order. New York, Alcestis Press, 1935.
Ideas of Order. New York, Alfred A. Knopf, 1936.
Owl's Clover. New York, Alcestis Press, 1936.
The Man With the Blue Guitar & Other Poems. New York, Alfred A. Knopf, 1937. Includes *Owl's Clover* in revised form.
Parts of a World. New York, Alfred A. Knopf, 1942.
Notes toward a Supreme Fiction. Cummington, Mass., The Cummington Press, 1942.
Esthétique du Mal. Cummington, Mass., The Cummington Press, 1944.
Transport to Summer. New York, Alfred A. Knopf, 1947. Includes *Notes toward a supreme Fiction* and *Esthétique du Mal.*
Three Academic Pieces. Cummington, Mass., The Cummington Press, 1947.
A Primitive Like an Orb. New York, Gotham Book Mart, 1948.

II. The Prose of Wallace Stevens

A. *Writings in Periodicals and Annuals*

"A Poet That Matters." *Life and Letters Today*, XIII (Dec., 1935), 61–65. On Marianne Moore's *Selected Poems*.

(On Eliot's poetry). *The Harvard Advocate*, CXXX (Dec., 1938), 41–42.

(Answers to a questionnaire). *Twentieth Century Verse*, XII–XIII (Oct., 1938), 107 and 112.

"Materia Poetica." *View*, I (Sept., 1940), 3.

Ibid., II (Oct., 1942), 28.

"The Figure of the Youth as Virile Poet." *Sewanee Review*, LII (Autumn, 1944), 508–29.

"Rubbings of Reality." *Briarcliff Quarterly*, III (Oct., 1946), 201–2. On Williams' poetry.

"John Crowe Ransom: Tennessean." *Sewanee Review*, LVI (Summer, 1948), 367–69.

(On the poem "The Emperor of Ice Cream" and the "meaning" of poetry). *The Explicator*, VII (Nov., 1948), 18.

"About One of Miss Moore's Poems." *Quarterly Review of Literature*, IV, 2 (1948), 143–49.

"Effects of Analogy," *The Yale Review*, XXXVIII (Sept., 1948), 29–44.

(Answer to questionnaire, "The Situation in American Writing"). *Partisan Review*, VI (Summer, 1939), 39–40.

(Answer to questionnaire, "The State of American Writing"), *ibid.*, XV (Aug., 1948), 884–86.

"Imagination as Value," *English Institute Annual*. New York, Columbia University Press, 1949.

B. *Anthologies and Other Books Containing Contributions by Stevens*

Williams, William Carlos. *Kora in Hell.* Boston, The Four Seas Company, 1920, pp. 17–18. Reprints a letter about Williams' poetry.

Benét, William Rose (ed.). *Fifty Poets.* New York, Duffield and Green, 1933, p. 46. On "The Emperor of Ice Cream."

Williams, William Carlos. *Collected Poems: 1921–1931.* New York, Objectivist Press, 1934, pp. 1–4. On Williams' poetry.

Benét, William Rose, and Pearson, Norman Holmes (eds.). *Oxford Anthology of American Literature.* New York, Oxford University Press, 1936, p. 1325. On Stevens' purpose in writing poetry.

Tate, Allen (ed.). *The Language of Poetry.* Princeton, Princeton University Press, 1942, pp. 91–125. "The Noble Rider and the Sound of Words."

Stevens, Wallace. *Parts of a World.* New York, Alfred A. Knopf, 1942. "The immense poetry of war. . . ."

Burnett, Whit (ed.). *This Is My Best.* New York, Dial Press, 1942, p. 652. On "Domination of Black."

Stevens, Wallace. *Three Academic Pieces.* Cummington, Mass., The Cummington Press, 1947, pp. 9–25. "The Realm of Resemblance."

Mellquist, Jerome (ed.). *Paul Rosenfeld: Voyager in the Arts.* New York, Creative Age, 1948, pp. 98–100. "The Shaper."

III. REVIEWS OF AND ARTICLES ABOUT STEVENS' POETRY

Baker, Howard. "Wallace Stevens and Other Poets," *Southern Review*, I (1935), 373–89.

Bewley, Marius. "The Poetry of Wallace Stevens," *Partisan Review*, XVI (Sept., 1949), 895–915.

Blackmur, R. P. "Examples of Wallace Stevens," *The Double Agent*. New York, Arrow Editions, 1935, pp. 68–102.

Breit, Harvey. "Sanity That Is Magic," *Poetry*, LXII (1943), 48–50.

Brinnin, John Malcolm. "Plato, Phoebus and the Man from Hartford," *Voices*, No. 121 (Spring, 1945), 30–37.

Cunningham, J. V. "The Poetry of Wallace Stevens," *Poetry*, LXXXV (1949), 149–65.

Ford, Charles Henri. "Verlaine in Hartford," *View*, I (Sept., 1940), 1 and 6.

Frankenberg, Lloyd. "Wallace Stevens," *Pleasure Dome*. Boston, Houghton Mifflin, 1949, pp. 197–267.

Gregory, Horace. "The Harmonium of Wallace Stevens," *A History of American Poetry, 1900–1940*. New York, Harcourt, Brace, 1942, pp. 326–35.

Hays, Hoffman R. "Laforgue and Wallace Stevens," *Romanic Review*, XXV (1934), 242–48.

Kreymborg, Alfred. *Our Singing Strength*. New York, Coward McCann, 1929, pp. 500–504.

Laros, Fred. "Wallace Stevens Today," *Bard Review*, II (Spring, 1947), 8–16.

Lowell, Robert. "Imagination and Reality," *The Nation*, CLXVI (Apr. 5, 1947), 400–402.

Martz, L. L. "Wallace Stevens: The Romance of the Precise," *Yale Poetry Review*, II (Aug., 1946), 13–20.

Matthiessen, F. O. "Poetry," *Literary History of the United States* (ed. Robert Spiller et al.). New York, Macmillan Co., 1948, II, 1354–55.

Monroe, Harriet. "Wallace Stevens," *Poets and Their Art*. New York, Macmillan Co., 1926, pp. 39–45.

Moore, Marianne. "Unanimity and Fortitude," *Poetry*, XLIX (1937), 268–72.

Munson, Gorham. "The Dandyism of Wallace Stevens," *Dial*, LXXIX (1925), 413–17.

Powys, Llewelyn. "The Thirteenth Way," *Dial*, LXXVII (1924), 45–50.

Ransom, John Crowe. "Poets Without Laurels," *The World's Body*. New York, Charles Scribner's Sons, 1938, pp. 55–75.

Rosenfeld, Paul. "Wallace Stevens," *Men Seen*. New York, Dial Press, 1925, pp. 151–62.

Simons, Hi. "The Comedian as the Letter C," *Southern Review*, V (1940), 453–68.

"The Humanism of Wallace Stevens," *Poetry*, LXI (1942), 448–52.

"The Genre of Wallace Stevens," *Sewanee Review*, LIII (1945), 566–79.

"Wallace Stevens and Mallarmé," *Modern Philology*, XLIII (1946), 235–59.

Symons, Julian. "A Short View of Wallace Stevens," *Life and Letters Today*, XXVI (1940), 215–24.

Sypher, Wylie. "Connoisseur in Chaos," *Partisan Review*, XIII (1946), 83–94.

Tate, Allen. "Wallace Stevens," *Sixty American Poets*. Washington, Library of Congress, 1945, pp. 156–57.

Taupin, René. *L'Influence du Symbolisme Français sur la Poèsie Américaine*. Paris, 1929, pp. 275–78.

Untermeyer, Louis. *American Poetry Since 1900*. New York, Henry Holt, 1923, pp. 323–28.

"The Wallace Stevens Number," *The Harvard Advocate* (Dec., 1940). Articles or brief comments by Allen Tate, Howard Baker, Cleanth Brooks, Harry Levin, F. O. Matthiessen, John Finch, Delmore Schwartz, Hi Simons, Marianne Moore, Theodore Spencer, William Carlos Williams, Robert Penn Warren, Morton D. Zabel.

Winters, Yvor. *Primitivism and Decadence* (New York, Arrow Editions, 1937), and "The Hedonist's Progress," in *The Anatomy of Nonsense* (Norfolk, Conn., New Directions, 1943); both reprinted in *The Defense of Reason*. New York, Swallow-Morrow, 1947, *passim*.

Zabel, Morton D. "The Harmonium of Wallace Stevens," *Poetry*, XXXIX (1931), 148–54.